LIMITED COMPANY FORMATION MADE EASY

Limited Company Formation Made Easy

ISBN 1 902646 43 6

Exclusion of Liability and Disclaimer

Table of contents

 # Introduction

This *Made Easy* Guide contains the information, instruction and examples of forms necessary to set up your own limited liability company. It is for people forming a company in England, Wales or Scotland. It is not suitable for Northern Ireland, nor for subsidiaries of overseas companies.

This Guide can help you achieve a business and legal objective conveniently, efficiently and economically. Nevertheless, it is important to use this Guide properly if you are to avoid later difficulties. Follow these guidelines:

1. This Guide contains all the basic instructions you need to complete forms which are reproduced in this Guide. If after thorough examination, you decide that your requirements are not met by this Guide, or you do not feel confident about completing your own documents, then consult a solicitor.

2. We have provided you with examples of the Companies House forms you will need to obtain and complete to set up your company. To help you run your company after incorporation, we have provided example formats of standard minutes, and completed examples of registers which are available from legal stationers.

3. Always use pen or type on legal documents; never use pencil.

4. Do not cross out or erase anything you have written on your final forms.

5. You will find a helpful glossary of terms in this Guide. Refer to this glossary if you find unfamiliar terms.

6. Always keep legal documents in a safe place. Registers, minutes, Memorandum and Articles of Association and the original Certificate of Incorporation should be kept at the company's registered office.

7. If you have any queries about what information should be filed with the Registrar of Companies, contact Companies House, Crown Way, Cardiff CF14 3UZ, tel: 01222 388 588 for companies registered in England and Wales. For information on Scottish companies, contact Companies House, 37 Castle Terrace, Edinburgh EH1 2EB, tel: 0131 535 5800. Companies House products and services are also detailed on its web site at: www.companieshouse.gov.uk.

Should you incorporate?

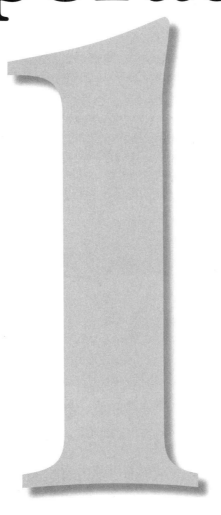

Chapter 1

Should you incorporate?

What you'll find in this chapter:

➠ What is a private company?

➠ Business entities

➠ Sole trader

➠ Partnership

➠ Shareholders liability

This Guide is intended for the entrepreneur who wants to incorporate a business. The demands of running or starting a business often prevent owners from carefully considering their options, assessing their situations and doing the necessary planning to organise their businesses to the best advantage.

In this Guide, the private limited company is compared and contrasted to two other business entities, the sole trader and the partnership. The structure, advantages and disadvantages of each are explained below. Completed examples of forms for incorporating your business are included, as well as step-by-step instructions for filling them in. In addition, valuable post-incorporation information about managing and changing your company's structure is included.

What is a private limited company?

A private limited company is:

DEFINITION

- A legal entity in its own right, distinct from its members.
- Owned by its members.
- Run by directors who are appointed by the members.
- Empowered to do anything contained in the objects clause of its charter, known as the Memorandum of Association.

If your company is limited by shares, your financial responsibility as a shareholder is limited to paying for your shares in full. This means that, provided you have paid for your shares in full, your personal assets cannot be touched, even if the company cannot pay its debts.

note If a shareholder subscibes £1,000 for one thousand £1 shares and the company becomes insolvent, owing millions of pounds in debt, the most he or she can lose is £1000.

Business entities

Whether you are currently running a business or planning to start a new enterprise, you should consider carefully the three basic types of business entity: sole trader, partnership and limited company. Each offers its own advantages and disadvantages.

A. Sole Trader

Operating as a sole trader is the simplest way of conducting a business. As a sole trader you are in charge of all aspects of the business. You are personally liable for all debts of the business, even in excess of the amount you invested. You and the business are considered to be the same entity.

The advantages of being a sole trader are:

1. There is no requirement to file accounts, annual returns or other information at Companies House (sometimes referred to as the Companies Registry), which means you have greater privacy. Companies House provides and handles the forms and documentation a company must fill out to comply with the law.

2. You are in complete control of the business and make all the business decisions.

3. There may be tax advantages.

4. You enjoy the greatest freedom from regulation and paperwork.

5. A sole trader receives all of the profits from the business.

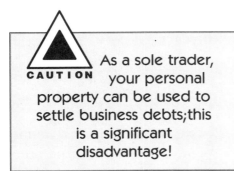

As a sole trader, your personal property can be used to settle business debts; this is a significant disadvantage!

The disadvantages of being a sole trader are:

1. You have unlimited liability and will be responsible for any amount of business debts no matter how incurred.

2. You may have difficulty in raising capital because you cannot transfer an interest in the business to investors as security for their investment.

3. The continuity of your business's existence cannot be ensured, as your death will terminate the business.

4. Since the name of the business is not registered, it cannot be protected without costly legal action.

B. Partnership

A partnership involves two or more individuals carrying on a business together with a view to profit. Each partner is personally liable for all debts of the partnership, including those incurred by the other partner(s). Partnership agreements can be quite complex.

The advantages of a partnership are:

1.   It has a broader management base than a sole trader.

2.   It may enjoy possible tax advantages by avoiding double taxation. The partnership pays corporation tax on its profit and the partners pay capital gains tax on the sale of their partnership shares, or income tax on dividends.

The disadvantages of a partnership are:

1.   The personal assets of each partner are available to satisfy any debts of the partnership. Therefore, each partner has unlimited liability.

> If you want to set up a partnership, you can use Law Pack's *Business Partnership Agreement* (F218), available from stationers and bookshops.

2.   The partnership may come to an end when existing partners leave or die. If there are two partners and one leaves or dies, the remaining partner becomes a sole trader.

3.   Obtaining large sums of capital is relatively difficult, as investment cannot be obtained from new shareholders.

4.   It may not be easy to sell or transfer an individual partnership interest.

5. Some tax incentives, such as employee share option schemes, are not available to partnerships.

C. Limited Company

Forming a limited company can be done individually or in concert with one or more investors or shareholders. A limited company is considered a separate legal entity with a distinct life of its own, separate from those of its members.

The advantages of a company are:

1. The shareholders have limited liability because they are not personally liable for the debts of the company: they need only pay for their shares in full. The shareholder's responsibility is limited to this amount, which is determined when the shareholder agrees to buy shares. Should the business fail, the creditors cannot obtain possession of shareholders' assets, such as homes or cars, in settlement of debts.

Despite the shield of limited liability, in certain circumstances directors may incur unlimited liability, for example, if they are found liable for either fraudulent trading or wrongful trading (see chapter 5, Liabilities of a director). Directors may also be liable to the company for any loss caused by their negligence or a breach of fiduciary duties.

Limited liability is the most important reason for so many businesses being incorporated.

2. Capital can be raised with relative ease because investors can buy shares in the company. This does not mean, however, that a new company can simply offer shares to the public. Share offers are regulated by law.

3. Subject to the Articles of Association, shares can be transferred to existing members and to family members as gifts or otherwise. It is

possible to sell your shares to other people, but not in a general offer to the public. Investors in a private company do not receive the same protection as they would have if they were investing in companies listed on The Stock Exchange.

4.   Unlike a partnership or a sole trader, which is dissolved upon the resignation, bankruptcy or death of a partner or owner, a limited company does not cease to exist simply because one of the shareholders dies or retires. Shares may change hands, personnel may change, but the company continues doing business. Thus, it is easier to ensure the continuity of a limited company than that of a partnership. Only dissolution of a company can end its legal existence.

5.   The name of the company is protected. The name is considered to be company property when registered with Companies House.

6.   There are clearly defined procedures for appointing, removing and retiring directors.

The disadvantages of a limited company are:

1.   It must comply with statutory rules and disclose information to the public.

2.   It is usually the most expensive form of business to organise and run, although a partnership can be equally expensive.

3.   Both the company and the individual shareholder have to make tax returns.

4.   Record keeping (such as keeping a minute book) can be more extensive for a company.

5.   Winding up a company and in many cases even changing its structure can be more complicated and expensive than for partnerships and sole traders.

> **TIP** The benefits of having limited liability and rising capital may not outweigh the disadvantages of higher costs, increased paperwork and greater regulation to which you will be subjected once you form a limited company.

The structure for your business should be considered carefully. Once you have decided that a limited company is the appropriate structure for your business, you must go through the legal steps required to create your limited company. With careful planning, most people can easily set up and run their own company without needing a solicitor, thus saving substantial legal fees.

Shareholders' liability

The liability of the shareholder is determined by the type of company formed:

1.   Private company limited by shares

The shareholder's liability is limited to the nominal value of the shares held by the shareholder. If the shareholder has agreed to pay more than the nominal value, the liability is for that greater sum. Provided the company is successful, the value of the shares will increase. If the company goes into liquidation, the shareholder can lose the entire investment.

2.   Private company limited by guarantee

If the company is wound up, the member's liability is limited to the amount the member has personally guaranteed to contribute to the assets of the company. This type of company has no share capital.

3.   Unlimited company

The shareholder's liability is not limited and the shareholder could be asked to pay the company's debts.

4.   Public limited company

The shareholder's liability is limited to the nominal value of the shares held by the shareholder. If the shareholder has agreed to pay more than the nominal value, liability is for that greater sum. On incorporation, the company's name and Memorandum of Association must specify that it is a public limited company. The statutory rules a public company must comply with are stricter than those that apply to private companies.

Creating and naming a private limited company

2

Chapter 2

Creating and naming a private limited company

What you'll find in this chapter:

⟱ Creating a private limited company

⟱ Naming your company

⟱ The registered office

Creating a private limited company

By following the instructions in this *Made Easy* Guide and photocopying and completing forms provided, and others available from Companies House (see page 81), you will be able to set up a private company limited by shares.

It will have:

- Two directors who are responsible for the management of the company.

- A company secretary, who may be one of the two directors. The secretary is responsible for the administration of the company and compliance with filing requirements.

- Authorised share capital of £100, made up of 100 shares, each with a nominal value of £1. It is possible to issue shares at a higher value so that the company has more capital (see chapter 6, The shareholders).

- A registered office in England or Wales, so that English law applies or in Scotland, so that Scottish law applies.

Because your company is a private limited company, it is not allowed to issue, or advertise for issue, any shares for sale to the public.

Note that all aspects of the company can be changed later, although certain formalities (and possibly fees) will be required. If you make any changes in the constitutional arrangements, you must notify Companies House.

The documents needed for incorporation, examples of which are included in this *Made Easy* Guide, are as follows:

1. Memorandum of Association sets out the name of the company, the location of the registered office, the objects for which the company was set up, the liability of the members and the authorised share capital.

2. Articles of Association contain the company's regulations for its internal management including the issuing of shares and a definition of the shareholders' relationship with the company and with each other. This document also defines the powers of the directors.

3. First directors and secretary and intended situation of registered office (Companies House Form 10) provides the address of the company's registered office and the names and addresses of the company secretary, directors, subscribers and the company agent.

4. Declaration on application for registration (Companies House Form 12) states that the directors have complied with all proper procedures to form a company.

A fifth requirement is the fee for incorporation. Companies House can advise on the current fee (tel. 01222 388 588 or 0131 535 5800).

Naming your company

Once you have chosen the kind of company you want to form, you must choose a company name and then determine whether you are allowed to use that name. The following points should be noted:

1. The name must include the word 'Limited' at the end of it. If you are incorporating a company in Wales (i.e. its registered office is in Wales), the name may be written in either English or Welsh. The Welsh word for 'Limited' is 'Cyfyngedig'. You can also use the abbreviations 'Ltd.' or 'Cyf'.

2. You cannot use a name for your company that:

    *   Is identical to a name already on the Register at Companies House;

    *   Is so similar as to be considered the same or too like a name on the Register.

For example:

(a)   Law Pack Publishing Limited
        Law Pack Publishing Company Limited

These two names would be considered the same.

(b)   Law Pack Publishing Limited
        Law Pak Publishing Limited

These names would not be refused initially as they are not identical. The lower company may have to change its name on a successful objection from upper company.

*   Is offensive or would constitute a criminal offence;
*   Is so misleading regarding the activities of the company as to cause

harm to the public;
- Gives the impression that the company is connected with H.M. Government or a local authority;
- Includes any of the sensitive words or expressions listed at the end of this Guide.

To obtain permission to use the name, you must first apply to Companies House:

The Registrar of Companies or	The Registrar of Companies
Companies House	Companies House
Crown Way	37 Castle Terrace
Cardiff CF14 3UZ	Edinburgh EH1 2EB
Tel: 01222 388588	Tel: 0131 535 5800

A name must be accepted before it is considered pending. Once your application is pending, you may arrange for a search of the index at the Registrar of Companies in London or at the above offices. If your name is acceptable, it is reserved pending confirmation by the company's shareholders, but the name cannot be used until the registrar issues the official certificate of incorporation. Companies have a target to incorporate in five days unless the name contains a sensitive word.

note

When a name is accepted for registration, it does not mean it can be used as a trade mark. Trade mark searches are separate and must be done at the Trade Marks Registry.

A company may, within 12 months of registration, be required by the Secretary of State to change its name if its registered name is the same as or too like that of another name on the register. If the Secretary of State considers that the registration was a result of misleading information, he or she may require the company to change its name at any time within five years of its incorporation. If you have any doubts about your choice of a name, consult Companies House.

Use of the company name

As soon as your company is incorporated, you are required to publish its name on business stationery and paint or affix the company name outside any office or place of business of your company. The name should be conspicuous and easily legible.

You must use your company name exactly as it appears on your Certificate of Incorporation. Remember to include the word 'Limited"' or 'Ltd'. If your company is registered in Wales and the company name includes the word 'Cyfyngedig' or 'Cyf.', you must state in English, on all business stationery and in the name displayed at the business premises, that the company is limited.

Your company name should appear on:

- All company business letters.
- All notices and other official publications.
- All bills of exchange, promissory notes, endorsements, cheques, and orders for money or goods to be signed by or on behalf of the company.
- All bills of parcels, invoices, receipts and letters of credit.

If the company's name does not appear on such documents, the person authorising such a document may be liable to a fine. If the company's name does not appear on a bill of exchange, cheque, etc., the person signing the instrument is liable to a fine and will become personally liable for the amount of the instrument, unless it is paid by the company.

You are required to specify the following additional information on your business letters and company order forms:

- Place of registration.
- Registration number, also called the company number (found on your Certificate of Incorporation).
- Registered office address (see over).

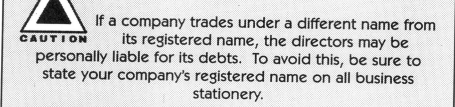

If a company trades under a different name from its registered name, the directors may be personally liable for its debts. To avoid this, be sure to state your company's registered name on all business stationery.

The registered office

This *Made Easy* Guide is only suitable for forming a company with a registered office in England, Wales or Scotland.

The purpose of a limited company's registered office is to enable the company to receive official notices and communications. The address also determines the tax office the company will deal with. Whilst the address of the company's main office is often used as the registered office, you could instead use the address of your solicitor or accountant, although he or she may make a charge for this.

Filling out the forms

Chapter 3
Filling out the forms

What you'll find in this chapter:

→ Memorandum of Association

→ Article of Association

→ Form 10

→ Form 12

In order to form your limited company, the following four documents must be completed and then filed together at Companies House: 1.**Memorandum of Association**, 2. **Articles of Association**, 3. **Form 10** and 4. **Form 12**.

 Note: You must be consistent with wording when referring to your company name on all documents filed at Companies House. Choose 'Limited' or 'Ltd.', but do not use both.

1) Memorandum of Association
(see page 82)

This is the company's charter, which lists all of the activities the company is entitled to do. Because a company that pursues activities outside its stated scope can run into problems, the Memorandum provided in this *Made Easy* Guide has been broadly drafted to give your company the right to conduct any trade or business whatsoever. In addition, the Memorandum provides for:

- Authorised capital of £100 divided into 100 shares of £1 each.
- Two subscribers (who become the first shareholders of the company), each to hold one share of £1 each.

To complete the Memorandum of Association:

- Select either the Memoradum for a company registered in England & Wales (see page 82) or the Memorandum for a company registered in Scotland (see page 84).
- You record the company's name in the two spaces provided.
- You state the number of shares to be taken by each subscriber and total number.
- Both subscribers state their names and addresses.
- Both subscribers sign the Memorandum above their respective names in the presence of a witness.
- The witness signs the Memorandum and states his/her name and address (and in Scotland, his or her occupation or designation as well).
- The Memorandum should be dated on the day it is signed.

2) Articles of Association
(see pages 86-89)

The Articles of Association are the rules by which the company must be run by the directors and shareholders. A standard set of rules which a private company limited by shares may adopt is provided by Table A of the Companies Act 1985. Table A consists of 118 standard articles designed for every type of company limited by shares, large public companies as well as small private ones. In this book you will find a modified set of Articles of Association based upon Table A, for use in both England & Wales and in Scotland.

Read the Articles of Association that have been provided to check that they are suitable for your company's needs. The most important of these is Article 25, which provides that when a person wants to transfer his shares in the company, he must first offer to sell them to existing shareholders. In addition, it gives the directors power to refuse to register any share transfer. Note also the provisions concerning quorums at general meetings (Article 41), meetings of the directors (Article 86) and director's interests in resolutions of the company (Articles 91 to 92).

If you do not understand any provisions in the Articles of Association or if any provision seems inappropriate for your company, you should consult a solicitor.

If you are satisfied with the Articles of Association included in this Law Pack Guide, you should carry out the following steps:

- Fill in the company's name in the space provided at the top of the first page of the Articles of Association.
- The two subscribers to the Memorandum must state their names and addresses at the end of the Articles.
- The two subscribers must sign and date the Articles in the presence of a witness, who must also sign as such and state his or her name and address.
- The Articles should be dated on the day of signing.

3) Form 10

(see page 92)

This is the statement of first directors and secretary and intended location of the registered office. You must provide the following:

- The company name.

- The address of the registered office.

- Personal details of the company secretary, including:
  (a) full name;
  (b) residential address.

- An address for correspondence.

- Personal details of the directors, including:
  (a) full name;
  (b) residential address;
  (c) date of birth;
  (d) nationality;
  (e) business occupation;
  (f) other directorships.

The secretary and each director must sign and date Form 10.

At the bottom of page 3 of Form 10 there are several signature boxes. Unless an agent is acting on your behalf, the two subscribers who signed the Memorandum must each sign and date the relevant boxes.

4) Form 12
(see page 96)

On this form, a director or secretary who has signed Form 10 makes an official declaration that all the requirements for registration of the company have been met. The declaration is self-explanatory and must be made and signed in the presence of a notary public, a commissioner for oaths (who can be a solicitor with a practising certificate) or a justice of the peace. Expect to pay a nominal fee for this.

After completing your forms and documents, send the Memorandum, Articles of Association, and Forms 10 and 12 together with a cheque for the fee payable to 'Companies House' to:

either	Registrar of Companies	or	Registrar of Companies
	Companies House		Companies House
	Crown Way		37 Castle Terrace
	Cardiff CF14 3UZ		Edinburgh EH1 2EB

Take copies of the forms before sending them, as Companies House charge for issuing copies of submitted forms. The registrar will then send you a Certificate of Incorporation. The company comes into existence from the date stated on the Certificate of Incorporation.

After incorporation

Chapter 4

After incorporation

Once your company is incorporated, there are certain legal requirements to be fulfilled and practical considerations to be dealt with.

To deal with these matters, you will need to hold a meeting of all the directors, which is called a board meeting. The decisions of all board meetings must be recorded in writing in what are known as the board 'minutes'. A specimen copy of board minutes, the Minutes of First Meeting of Directors, is provided at the end of this Guide. In lieu of attending a board meeting, all the directors can sign a Written Resolution of Directors, an example of which is also provided at the end of this Guide.

This chapter discusses what should be decided, whether at a board meeting or by written resolution.

The number and distribution of shares

The directors should issue and allot one share worth £1 each to each of the subscribers to the Memorandum. A majority of the directors must agree to do so at the board meeting or by written resolution.

Companies House must be notified within one month of the allotment. Notification is given by obtaining, completing and filing Return of Allotments of Shares, Form G88(2). The completed example in this book provides for the issue of one share to each of two subscribers. Complete Form G88(2) according to your own requirements.

The register of members should be completed by the secretary to show the two subscribers as members of the company. The registers of directors, secretaries, and directors' interests should also be completed. Sample registers are provided in this book and are discussed more fully later in this chapter.

To provide the shareholders with a title document to their shares, you will need to issue share certificates at the first board meeting. Each share certificate must include the following:

- A certificate number.
- The name of the company.
- The name of the holder.
- The address of holder.
- The number and type of shares issued to the holder.
- The nominal value of the shares.
- A statement of the extent to which the shares are paid up.

This *Made Easy* Guide contains a blank share certificate for photocopying and use.

If you have a company seal, it can be stamped on the certificate in the presence of two directors, or one director and the company secretary, and its use authorised by their signatures. If you do not have a seal, the certificate can merely be signed as above. The certificate should be dated on issue.

Opening a bank account and appointing auditors

The directors must approve the opening of a company bank account either at a board meeting or by written resolution.

The company is obliged by law to file annual audited accounts (i.e. audited by a chartered accountant). The directors must pass a resolution appointing auditors, who must be independent of the company (for example, not employees of the company).

note Unless you change it, your accounting reference date will automatically fall on the last day of the month in which the anniversary of the company's incorporation falls.

Your company will need to prepare accounts for each financial year. Your first financial year may be shorter or longer than twelve months: it will begin on the date of incorporation and end on the last day of its 'accounting reference' period.

To change the accounting reference date you must give notice to the Registrar of Companies by obtaining and using Form 225. To help you complete Form 225, we have provided a completed sample form. The company's first accounting reference period is fixed as the last day in the month in which the anniversary of its incorporation occurs. Thereafter, company can change its accounting reference date either during its current accounting period, or during the period allowed for delivering the accounts in question. A company cannot extend an accounting period more than once in five years unless certain circumstances apply (see 'Notes' in completed example). You should fill in the following:

- Company number (the registration number found on the certificate of incorporation)
- Name of company.
- Day and month and year of the company's shortened or extended accounting reference period.

In addition, the form must be signed by either a director or the company secretary, and you should indicate which by signing accordingly. Date the form and write the company's name and address in the box provided to enable Companies House to correspond with you.

The transfer of assets

If you have been operating a business prior to incorporation, you can transfer the assets and debts of that business to the new company at an agreed sum and receive shares in the new company.

You may not, however, burden your company with more debt than assets. You may not sell your personal property to the company at inflated prices, or exchange company shares for personal property that is overvalued. If a director wishes to buy a non-cash asset from the company or dispose of such an asset to the company, and that asset is above a certain statutory value, the shareholders must approve the transaction in a general meeting or by written resolution. Your accountant can advise you on this. You will also need

to consult your solicitor on how to effect the transfer of your assets to the company.

The directors will need to execute a formal transfer agreement and an appropriate resolution, which must be documented in the board minutes. Stamp duty may be payable on documents relating to the transfer of assets (e.g. property).

Taxation issues

You will need to contact your local tax office if you are employing staff, including paid directors who are employees of the company. It will provide the documents required to operate a PAYE (pay as you earn) scheme and tell you how to make national insurance contributions.

You should contact H.M. Customs and Excise to find out whether you need to register for VAT (Value Added Tax):

HM Customs and Excise   or   HM Customs and Excise
King's Beam House   Caledonian House
39–41 Mark Lane   Greenmarket
London EC3R 7HE   Dundee DD1 1HD
Tel 020 7626 1515   Tel 01382 200 822

Your accountant will be able to help you with queries concerning corporation tax and capital gains tax.

Other business

Other business conducted at the first board meeting:

- The chairperson or managing director should be appointed.
- Additional directors may be appointed.
- The company seal (if any) should be adopted.
- The company's official signatories should be appointed.
- Solicitors should be appointed.
- The company should decide whether to keep the current registered office or change its location.
- Directors' interests in company contracts must be disclosed.

Statutory books

You must maintain certain records about directors, shareholders and the company's meetings. These records, known as statutory books, are kept for the benefit of the shareholders and the general public.

In this *Made Easy* Guide you will find completed examples of registers, available from legal stationers. These include:

1. **Register of Members.** This register lists the names and addresses of all members, along with detailed descriptions of their holdings. Entries can be removed only after a person has not held shares for 20 years.

2. **Register of Directors.** This register maintains the records of forenames, surnames, former names, residential addresses, nationalities and occupations of directors. In addition, it details any other directorships a person has held within the last five years.

3. **Register of Secretaries.** This records the secretary's name, former name (if any) and residential address.

4. **Register of Directors' Interests.** This records the directors' interests in shares or debentures of the company and its associated companies together with any interest of a director's spouse or child.

5. **Register of Charges.** This records charges over the property of the company (example not included).

Each of the registers should be kept at the company's registered office. You should complete all the information requested on the forms. Shareholders can inspect the statutory books free of charge, but the company may charge anyone else a nominal fee for inspection.

note

Your accountant will be able to advise you on the accounting records that need to be kept. In addition, copies of the directors' service contracts, if any, and copies of any charges (for example, loans secured on the company's assets) must be kept by the company and be available for inspection by any member of the company.

Minute book. You are legally required to keep a record of board and shareholder meetings. Although this record is referred to as a minute book, it may take the form of an ordinary file. Board meetings and shareholder meetings must be fully recorded in writing. Written resolutions must also be noted in a minute book. The minutes must be signed by a director or chairman and filed. The company must maintain a continuous and up-to-date record of all actions approved by shareholders and/or directors.

Company seal

note Whether or not the company has a seal, a document that is signed by a director and the secretary or by two directors of the company 'on behalf of such and such Company Limited' has the same effect as if it were executed under the seal of the company.

There is no longer a legal obligation to have a company seal. If you decide to have a company seal, one can be ordered from a legal stationer. The seal is stamped on a document and witnessed by a director and the secretary or by two directors of the company. Use of the seal should be authorised by the board (see Article 98 of the Articles).

Annual duties

Annual return

Your company must deliver an annual return to Companies House relating to all business carried out up to the anniversary of the company's incorporation. It must be in the form prescribed by Companies House, Form 363, and must be signed by a director or secretary of the company. This form is automatically sent to companies shortly before the annual return is due. Once the form is completed, the same information will be repeated the following year unless the company amends it. The information you will need to complete this form consists of: the company's name and number (which appears on your Certificate of Incorporation), the address of the registered office, type of company, main business activity and names, addresses, and dates of birth of directors.

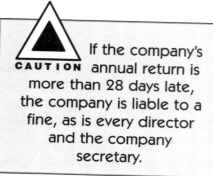

If the company's annual return is more than 28 days late, the company is liable to a fine, as is every director and the company secretary.

Annual accounts

The company must file its annual accounts, consisting of a balance sheet and a profit-and-loss account made up to the last day of the company's financial year. The company must file a directors' report and an auditor's report with each set of annual accounts. The accounts must be delivered to Companies House within 10 months after the end of the relevant accounting reference period. The company and each director is liable to a fine if the company fails to file such accounts.

The accounts must be approved by the directors and signed on behalf of the board by a director. The directors' report must be approved by the directors and signed on behalf of the board by a director or the secretary. The auditor's report must be signed by the auditors.

note If a company trades in Wales, the accounts may be in Welsh, but a certified English translation must be attached when they are submitted to Companies House.

With certain exceptions, a company may qualify for a more relaxed accounting regime if it qualifies as a 'small company'. In summary, a small company must have two of the following three characteristics:

1. Turnover not exceeding £2.8 million.

2. A balance sheet not exceeding £1.4 million.

3. An average number of employees not exceeding 50.

If it qualifies it may deliver an 'abbreviated' balance sheet and need not deliver a profit and loss account or a directors' report at all. If, in addition, the company has a turnover not exceeding £350,000 and its balance sheet total does not exceed £1.4 million it will be totally exempt from the requirements of having an audit.

In any case, members holding not less than 10% in nominal value of any class of shares may, by written notice, not later than one month before the end of a financial year, require the company to obtain an audit for that year. Annual accounts must be submitted in English.

TIP Consult Companies House if you have any queries concerning the information to be filed.

Remember, the company must notify Companies House of changes to the company's constitution, share capital and management.

Elective resolutions

Annual General Meetings of shareholders (AGMs) must be held to lay the annual accounts and directors' and auditor's reports before the shareholders and to deal with other matters, such as the annual appointment of auditors. However, private companies can pass elective resolutions dispensing with the laying of accounts and reports before the shareholders, the annual appointment of auditors and Annual General Meetings. This Law Pack Guide includes examples of such elective resolutions passed as written resolutions of shareholders. These are for reference when preparing your own.

Where the company has passed an elective resolution dispensing with the laying of accounts and reports before the shareholders, the shareholders must be provided with a printed copy of the company's annual accounts together with the directors' report and the auditor's report. Shareholders are entitled to receive the above documents at least 28 days before the accounts are due to be delivered to Companies House. Shareholders must be informed of their right to require the laying of accounts and reports before the General Meeting and any shareholder can enforce this right.

Management of the company

5

Chapter 5

Management of the company

The following background information will help you understand how to run your company.

Company directors

DEFINITION

Company directors may be known as 'executive', 'managing' or 'first' directors. The directors' responsibility is to run the company on behalf of the shareholders. Anyone can be a director except a person disqualified by a court order, a clergyman or an undischarged bankrupt. In public companies or their subsidiaries only, someone over the age of 70 is disqualified from being a director unless the appointment is approved in general meeting by an ordinary resolution, of which 'special notice' stating his or her age has been given.

It should be noted that a person cannot act as both a director of the company and the company's auditor. The company secretary cannot be a sole director of a private company (and where something has to be done by the director and the secretary, the same person cannot act in both capacities). The Articles included with this guide cause a director to vacate office if he or she is of unsound mind, or misses more than six months of board meetings without the consent of the board.

Directors have extensive powers delegated by the shareholders in the Articles of Association. But shareholders can dismiss directors by following specific procedures and passing an ordinary resolution at a meeting of shareholders. Shareholders holding a simple majority (either alone or collectively with other shareholders) of the issued shares of the company will be able to remove a director and control the composition of the board. Notice must be given to the company at least 28 days before the intended meeting and the company must give notice forthwith to each director concerned. The company must also give notice of such a resolution, to the members, at least 21 days before the meeting.

Directors are obliged to act in good faith and in the best interests of the company . They must avoid placing themselves in a position where there is, or might be, a conflict between their personal interest and their duty to the company. They must exercise skill and care in their role as directors and observe the limitations and procedures of the company's Memorandum and Articles of Association and the statutory provisions applying to companies.

> **note**
> Sometimes the directors and shareholders are the same people, although there is no requirement that they should be.

Board meetings

The day-to-day management of the company will generally be carried out by the directors. Decisions are taken at board meetings, which are conducted with the following requirements:

1. The Articles specify that at least two directors must be present at board meetings.

2. All the directors in the UK must receive reasonable notice of a board meeting (see Article 85). Resolutions are passed by a majority of the directors at the board meeting. The example limited company in this guide has two directors and does not provide the chairman with a casting vote (i.e. a second vote used to break a tie, in addition to his/her director's vote). Should your company grow and the number of directors increase, you may want to amend your Articles to include a chairman's casting vote to avoid a possible impasse at board meetings.

3. A record of board meetings must be kept. This record is known as the board minutes.

4. If the directors do not wish to hold a board meeting, they can pass a written resolution provided all directors sign that resolution (see Article 90). The resolution is dated when the last director signs it and it is entered in the minute book.

Appointment of directors

The initial directors may be appointed in two ways:

1. By being named in the incorporation documents (Form 10) filed at Companies House.

2. By being appointed in the Articles of Association of the company.

As well as directors who are appointed by the company, there may be persons who act as if they were directors of the company but who are not properly appointed as such. As such persons might incur liabilities (both for themselves and the company), such situations should be avoided. Further, other persons may act as a 'shadow director', that is a person in accordance with whose directions or instructions the directors of the company are accustomed to act. However, advice given in a professional capacity does not make the adviser a shadow director. Shadow directors may find themselves subject to the same obligations and liabilities as properly appointed directors.

A director's contract

The fact that a person is a director of the company does not make him or her an employee of the company. Since directors have no rights to remuneration under the Articles themselves, their employment should be governed by an employment contract. This contract should lay down all of the terms and conditions of employment, including but not limited to benefits, life assurance, pension, remuneration and compensation for loss of office.

The terms of a company's employment contract with its directors (or any shadow director) must be made available for inspection by the members. If an agreement is made whereby a director (or shadow director) is to provide services to the company for more than five years and it contains a term under which the company cannot terminate the employment by notice (or can only do so in specified circumstances), then that term is void and the company is deemed to be able to terminate the contract on reasonable notice, unless the agreement receives the prior approval of the company in general meeting.

Duties of the director

The main duties of any directors are:

1. To exercise their powers in the best interests of the company as a whole and for a proper purpose.

2. To act with such care as would reasonably be expected of someone in such a position (although if directors do have some special skill

relevant to the company's business, then they are bound to give the company the advantage of their additional experience).

3. To abide by and fulfil the legal obligations set out in the Companies Acts and other relevant legislation.

4. To avoid conflicts of duty (in a broad sense) between their personal positions and the position of the company.

Liabilities of a director

Although a director's personal liability is shielded by the limited liability of the company, there may be circumstances when such a shield does not apply, for example, in cases of fraudulent or wrongful trading, or in the case of a director giving personal guarantees.

A person who is found to have been knowingly involved in the carrying on of the business of a company with intent to defraud creditors of the company, or creditors of any other person, or for any fraudulent purpose, may be liable to make such contribution to the company's assets as the court thinks proper. A director or shadow director of the company may be similarly liable to contribute to the assets of any insolvent company if the director knew, or ought to have concluded, that there was no reasonable prospect of the company avoiding insolvent liquidation.

A director will be liable (in accordance with the terms of such guarantees) for any personal guarantees voluntarily given in order that the company be able to secure a business lease or certain types of commercial contract.

In addition, directors can be disqualified by the court in a number of circumstances.

Company secretary

> **TIP** For more information on filing requirements and on the role of company secretaries, consult *Company Minutes & Resolutions Made Easy*, a source of more than 125 everyday, ready-made resolutions and notices for company record-keepers.

Your company must have a' secretary' (in the sense of a record-keeper rather than a typist or PA). The secretary and the directors are responsible for keeping the company's registers and minutes and for filing information at Companies House. The secretary also attends the meetings of directors and shareholders to record the minutes. The first secretary is appointed on incorporation, and is documented in Form 10. The board can also pass resolutions to appoint or remove a secretary.

The shareholders

Chapter 6

The shareholders

The company consists of two or more shareholders who own shares. A company is incorporated with an authorised share capital. In this Guide the authorised share capital is £100, and each share has a nominal value of £1.

When a company is incorporated, it issues shares to shareholders. These shares are paid for with money, property or services. If, for example, shareholders applied for two shares and these were issued, you would say that the company had an issued share capital of £2 and an authorised share capital of £100. The directors can issue the remaining 98 shares comprising the authorised share capital. Provided that the shareholders have passed an ordinary resolution to increase the share capital, the directors can issue the shares comprising the increased share capital. The authority in the *Made Easy Guide* Articles permits the directors to issue shares up to a maximum nominal amount of £10,100.

Note that the authority expires five years after the date of incorporation.

If shares are to be allotted for cash, statutory rules governing the manner and timing of such an offer require that shares be offered to existing shareholders in proportion to their shareholdings. If you want to exclude these rules (e.g. if you want to offer shares to a new shareholder), you should consult a solicitor. In the example company in this *Made Easy Guide*, only two shares have been issued.

Capital of the company

DEFINITION

It is possible to issue shares of the company at a price greater than their nominal value, to bring more money into the company while protecting the voting rights of existing shareholders, and avoiding the procedures required to increase the authorised share capital of the company. For example, £1 shares could be sold for £10, with the difference between the actual and nominal value of each share (£10 – £1 = £9) being held in a separate account, known as a 'share premium account'.

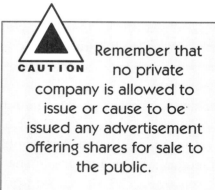

Remember that no private company is allowed to issue or cause to be issued any advertisement offering shares for sale to the public.

Once the directors have issued all the shares in the authorised capital (in the case of this *Made Easy Guide* company, £100), no additional shares may be issued unless the share capital is increased by an ordinary resolution of the shareholders. In addition, the shareholders must authorise the directors to allot any shares represented by the increased capital if it exceeds £10,100.

In this *Made Easy* Guide, the rights attached to ordinary shares entitle the holders to receive notice of shareholders' meetings and to speak and vote at such meetings. On a poll, each share carries one vote. Shareholders are entitled to any dividends declared by the company and to a proportion of the company's assets on its dissolution.

The shares may be paid for, nil paid (unpaid) or partly paid for on issue. If they are partly paid for or nil paid, the company will be entitled to ask for the balance owed on each share and the shareholder must pay it.

Transfer of shares

Having been issued shares in your company, the shareholders are permitted to sell their shares or give them away, but they may only transfer their shares in accordance with the Articles of Association. The Articles in this Guide require shareholders to appoint the company as their agent for the transfer of shares (see Article 25). The company is obliged to offer the transfer shares to the existing shareholders. If the company fails to find a purchaser among the existing shareholders within 28 days, the selling shareholder is free to sell his or her shares to outsiders (subject always to the directors' power to refuse to register a transfer of shares). There are provisions for dealing with the negotiation of a fair price for the shares within this clause.

Shareholders' meetings

Most of the day-to-day running of the company is carried out by the directors, so the shareholders will not need to worry about the following unless it is a very important issue (for example, issues concerning capital or the company's constitution). In some cases directors and shareholders will be the same people.

> **note**
>
> Shareholders act officially as a group. This means that either a formal meeting or a written resolution signed by all the shareholders is necessary before it can legally bind the company. If you do not wish to hold a meeting and want to act by written resolution, use the example format in this Guide.

Certain rules and procedures have to be followed in order to call and conduct a shareholders' meeting:

A. Notice.

Shareholders must receive advance warning of meetings.

1. Each shareholder entitled to attend the meeting must receive notice of all meetings (see Articles 39 and 40). Each should be notified of the date, time, place and the details of the proposed resolutions to be considered at the meeting.

2. Each shareholder must receive his or her own notice of the meeting. The length of notice depends upon the type of resolutions proposed:

    (a)   In the case of an Annual General Meeting or a general meeting at which a special resolution is proposed, at least 21 clear days' notice should be given.

    (b)   In the case of a general meeting other than those specified above, at least 14 clear days' notice should be given. All general meetings other than annual meetings are called Extraordinary General Meetings. An example Notice of Extraordinary General Meeting (EGM) is included in this *Made Easy* Guide.

    (c)   It is also possible for meetings to be held at short notice provided the requisite majority of shareholders have consented to short notice. This consent is recorded and signed in writing. In most cases you will be able to hold the meeting immediately if you obtain the shareholders' consent to short notice. An example format of a Consent to Short Notice is included in this *Made Easy* Guide.

Consent to short notice may be given:

- In the case of an Annual General Meeting, by all the members entitled to attend and vote at the meeting.

- In the case of other general meetings, by a majority in number of the members holding not less than 95 per cent in nominal value of the shares and having the right to attend and vote at the meeting (or 90 per cent if an elective resolution to that effect has been passed).

B. Proxies.

DEFINITION

If unable to attend, each shareholder may appoint someone to attend the meeting on his/her behalf (a 'proxy'). The proxy may attend and speak at the meeting and vote on a poll on the shareholder's behalf (see Articles 60–64). The proxy may not vote on a show of hands.

The notice calling the meeting should inform shareholders that they are entitled to appoint a proxy to attend and vote in their place, and that the proxy need not be a shareholder.

The proxy form must be lodged with the company within a specified period before the meeting is held (this period cannot be longer than 48 hours). See Articles 61 and 62 for specimen proxy forms.

C. Quorum.

DEFINITION

Shareholders act collectively, not individually, so a certain number of shareholders must be present before a meeting can be held. This is known as a 'quorum'.

Article 41 provides for a minimum of two shareholders present, either in person or by proxy, to be a quorum. Resolutions are passed by the requisite majority of those voting shareholders present at shareholders meetings (and on a poll whether present in person or by proxy).

Should your company grow and the number of shareholders increase, you may want to amend your Articles to include a chairman's casting vote to avoid a possible impasse at shareholders' meetings.

D. Voting.

Shareholders vote to make their collective decisions. The vote that takes place at the meeting can be made in one of two ways:

1. On a show of hands — every shareholder present (excluding proxies) is entitled to cast one vote.

2. On a poll — every shareholder present is entitled to cast one vote for every share held. Proxies may vote on a poll. For information on how to demand a poll, see Article 47.

The number of votes required to pass a particular item depends on whether the resolution is 'ordinary' or 'special'.

*   **Ordinary resolutions.** Ordinary resolutions proposed at a general meeting must be approved by a simple majority (i.e. more than 50 per cent) of the votes cast at the meeting, whether by a show of hands or on a poll. Examples of business that must be approved by ordinary resolution include:

    (a)   Increasing the share capital. You also must file Form G123 (completed example provided in this Guide) at Companies House.

    (b)   Removal of a director.

There are many more instances when an ordinary resolution is required. Those instances are not covered here. The above is merely to give you an example of the sort of business which is transacted by shareholders rather than by directors.

- **Special resolutions**. Special resolutions must be passed by a three-quarters majority of the votes cast at the meeting, whether by a show of hands or on a poll.

Examples of business that must be approved by special resolution are:

(a) Alteration to the Memorandum of Association.

(b) Alteration to the Articles of Association.

(c) Reduction of capital.

(d) A change of name – you also must send the appropriate fee to Companies House.

There are many more instances when a special resolution is required. Those instances are not covered here.

Some ordinary and all special resolutions must be filed at Companies House within 15 days of passage. Sometimes forms and fees must accompany the resolutions (e.g. Form G123).

Written resolutions

In most cases, it is possible (and less complicated) for the shareholders to pass a written resolution rather than hold a meeting. A written resolution must be signed by or on behalf of all shareholders entitled to attend and vote at the meeting. No notice of the proposed resolution is required, although a copy of the proposed resolution must be supplied to and considered by the company's auditors.

The auditors must express their opinion that it does not concern them as auditors, or that it does concern them, but need not be considered by the company in general meeting; alternatively, the auditors can fail to express such opinion within seven days of their receipt of the copy of the notice.

An example of written resolutions appears in this Guide. Written resolutions that would not have been effective unless passed as special resolutions, and some other written resolutions, must be filed at Companies House within 15 days of being passed. A record of the written resolution (and the signatures) must be entered in the company's minute book.

Post-incorporation changes

7

Chapter 7

Post-incorporation changes

What you'll find in this chapter:

- Appointment of removal of the company secretary
- Appointment or removal of auditors
- Location of the registered office
- The name of the company
- Increase in company capital
- Allotting shares
- The object clause
- The Articles of Association
- The accounting reference date

It is possible to make changes to the corporate structure after you have successfully set up your company. However, there are strict procedural formalities that must be followed. Companies House must always be kept informed of corporate changes; failure to file the proper documentation will result in penalties.

The most common post-incorporation changes involve:

1. **Appointment or removal of the company secretary.**

This decision is made by the company directors. It is not necessary for the shareholders to vote on this issue, but Companies House must be notified of any change.

2. **Appointment or removal of auditors.**

Normally, an auditor is appointed at the Annual General Meeting and serves until the next such meeting. If the auditor decides to resign, he must deposit notice with the company, indicating whether there are circumstances that ought to be drawn to the attention of members or creditors of the company (or not), and the company must deposit such notice with Companies House. If there are circumstances which the auditor considers should be drawn to the attention of members or creditors, a copy of the auditor's statement must be sent to each member or the company apply to court. The resigning auditor may also require the company to convene an Extraordinary General Meeting to provide his comments to members, and can require the company to circulate his written comments in advance of the meeting.

A company may remove an auditor from office by an ordinary resolution. If this resolution would be passed before the expiry of the auditor's term of office, 28 days' notice is required. Notice must be given to the auditor who it is proposed to remove and to the person whom it is proposed to appoint. An auditor proposed to be removed or retiring without being proposed for re-appointment is entitled to make written representations to the company and to have these circulated to members or read out at the general meeting.

3. **Location of the registered office.**

If the company wants to change the location of the registered office, or of the statutory books and other documents open to the public, Companies House must be notified within 14 days of the change.

4. **The name of the company.**

A majority of shareholders must vote for a special resolution to change the name of the company. This special resolution must be filed with Companies House within 15 days of the meeting.

5. **Increase in company capital.**

A company may increase its authorised share capital by an ordinary resolution passed at a general meeting (and not by a written resolution). On an increase in capital, the directors will be unable to allot the newly created shares unless authority is conferred on them (by ordinary resolution) to allot such shares (see 6 below). Within 15 days of the passing of the resolution by the company, a notice (on Form G123) must be delivered to Companies House together with a copy of the revised Memorandum.

6. **Allotting shares.**

Altering directors' authority to allot shares requires a majority adoption of an ordinary resolution at a general meeting. A copy of that resolution must be sent to Companies House within 15 days of its adoption.

7. **The objects clause.**

If the company desires to change its objects clause and thus its Memorandum of Association, 75 per cent of the shareholders must agree to a special resolution.

8. **The Articles of Association.**

The Articles of Association may be altered by a majority of 75 per cent of the shareholders voting on a special resolution.

9. **The accounting reference date.**

If a change is made to the accounting reference date, details of the change must be submitted to Companies House before the end of the accounting period.

Glossary

DEFINITION

Accounting reference date — the annual anniversary upon which the company's financial year ends.

Accounting reference period — the period which ends on the accounting reference date.

Allotment — the appropriation by the board of shares in the capital of the company to the holders of shares.

Articles of Association — the document containing the company's regulations for its internal management.

Assets — anything owned of monetary value, including both real and personal property.

Authorised capital — the nominal capital which the company is authorised to issue by its Memorandum of Association. This capital may be increased by subsequent resolution.

Board — a quorum of the company's directors acting together to determine and carry out company policy.

Board meeting — a meeting of the company's directors.

Director — an officer of the company who manages the business conducted by the company.

Elective resolution — a resolution that a private company is entitled to pass to reduce or remove certain administrative or formal requirements and requiring the consent of all those shareholders entitled to vote.

General Meeting — an Annual General Meeting or an Extraordinary General Meeting where shareholders give their approval for transactions.

Incorporate — to form a limited company by following procedures prescribed by law. On incorporation the limited company becomes a separate legal entity in its own right distinct from its owners.

DEFINITION

Issued shares — the number of shares issued by the company to its shareholders.

Member — someone who is a subscriber or who has agreed to become a member of the company and whose name is entered in the Register of Members.

Memorandum of Association — the company's charter defining the extent of the company's powers.

Minutes — written records of formal proceedings of shareholders' and directors' meetings.

Poll — ascertaining the will of the shareholders at a general meeting of the company by counting shareholders' votes according to the size of their shareholding. On a poll a proxy may vote.

Pre-emption — the right of existing shareholders granting them first option to acquire shares which are to be transferred or issued in proportion to their present shareholding.

Proxy — shareholder's authorisation appointing another to attend a meeting to speak and vote on his behalf. A proxy may also be the person so authorised.

Quorum — the number of shareholders or directors who must be present before a meeting can be held.

Registered office — the postal address of the company, which is notified to Companies House as the registered office.

Resolution — decision made by directors or shareholders in accordance with requisite majorities set out in Articles of Association. Resolutions are approved in meetings or in writing.

Share certificate — written and executed instrument showing who holds title to a particular share or series of shares.

DEFINITION

Shareholder — someone who holds shares in the company.

Statutory books — the records that a company must keep as required by law. Changes must be notified to the Registrar of Companies at Companies House. These records are available for public inspection.

Subscriber — a person who signs the Memorandum of Association.

Written resolution — a resolution passed either by the shareholders or the directors of the company by signing a written form of the resolution rather than being at a general meeting of the company or at a meeting of the directors of the company.

List of sensitive words

Sensitive words

The use of a company or business name that includes any of the following words will require the approval of the Secretary of State for Trade and Industry.

Association	Federation	Patentee
Assurance	Foundation	Post Office
Assurer	Friendly Society	Reassurance
Authority	Fund	Reassurer
Benevolent	Giro	Register
Board	Great Britain	Registered
British	Group	Reinsurance
Chamber of Commerce	Holding	Reinsurer
Chamber of Industry	Industrial &	Scotland
Chamber of Trade	Provident Society	Scottish
Charter	Institute	Sheffield
Chartered	Institution	Society
Chemist	Insurance	Stock Exchange
Chemistry	Insurer	Trade Union
Co-operative	International	Trust
Council	Ireland	United Kingdom
England	Irish	Wales
English	National	Welsh
European		

The use of a company or business name which includes any of the following words or expressions requires the Secretary of State's approval (see chapter 3). A written request must be made seeking the opinion of the relevant body as to the use of the word or expression. A copy of any response received will be required before approval is sought from the Secretary of State.

Word or Expression	Relevant body in England and Wales	Relevant body in Scotland
Charity, Charitable	Charity Commission Registration Division St Albans House 57–60 Haymarket London SW1Y 4QX	Inland Revenue Claims Branch Trinity Park House South Trinity Road Edinburgh EH5 3SD
or		
For businesses **NOT** intending to register as a charity	Charity Commission 2nd Floor 20 Kings Parade Queens Dock Liverpool L3 4DQ	
Contact Lens	General Optical Council 41 Harley Street London W1N 2DJ	As for England and Wales
Dental, Dentistry	General Dental Council 37 Wimpole Street London W1M 8DQ	As for England and Wales
District Nurse, Health Visitor, Midwife, Midwifery, Nurse, Nursing	UK Central Council for Nursing, Midwifery and Health Visiting 23 Portland Place London W1N 3JT	As for England and Wales

Word or Expression	Relevant body in England and Wales	Relevant body in Scotland
Health Centre	Department of Health & Social Security . 48 Carey Street London WC2A 2LS	As for England and Wales
Health Service	Department of Health Eileen House 80-94 Newington Causeway London SE1 6EF	As for England and Wales
Police	Home Office Police Department Strategy Group Room 510 50 Queen Anne's Gate London SW1H 9AT	Scottish Home and Health Department Police Division St Andrews House Regent Road Edinburgh EH1 3DG
Polytechnic	Department for Education and Science FHE 1B Sanctuary Buildings Great Smith Street Westminster London SW1P 3BT	As for England and Wales
Pregnancy, Termination, Abortion	Department of Health Area 423 Wellington House 133-155 Waterloo Road London SE1 8UG	As for England and Wales

Word or Expression	Relevant body in England and Wales	Relevant body in Scotland
	If based in England:	
Royal, Royale, Royalty, King, Queen, Prince, Princess, Windsor, Duke, His/Her Majesty	Home Office A Division Room 730 50 Queen Anne's Gate London SW1H 9AT	Scottish Office Home Department Civil Law and Legal Aid Division Saughton House Broomhouse Drive Edinburgh EH11 3XD
	If based in Wales:	
	Welsh Office Crown Buildings Cathays Park Cardiff CF1 3NQ	
Special School	Department for Education and Employment Schools 2 Branch Sanctuary Buildings Great Smith Street Westminster London SW1P 3BT	As for England and Wales
University	Privy Council Office 68 Whitehall London SW1A 2AT	As for England and Wales

The use of certain words in company or business names is covered by other legislation, and may constitute a criminal offence. Some of these words are listed below, but the list is not exhaustive. Owners of a business wishing to use any of these words should obtain confirmation from the appropriate body that the use of the word does not contravene the relevant legislation.

Word or Expression	Appropriate body
Anzac	Seek advice of Companies House
Architect, Architectural	Architects Registration Council of the United Kingdom 73 Hallam Street London W1N 6EE
Bank, Banker, Banking Deposit	Bank of England Supervision and Surveillance Threadneedle Street London EC2R 8AH
Building Society	Building Societies Commission Victoria House 30–34 Kingsway London WC2B 6ES
*Chiropodist, *Dietician, *Medical Laboratory Technician, *Occupational Therapist, *Orthoptist, *Physiotherapist, *Radiographer, *Remedial Gymnast	Room 12.26 HAP4 Division Department of Health Hannibal House Elephant and Castle London SE1 6TE

Where preceded by the words Registered, State Registered, State

Word or Expression	Appropriate body
Credit Union	Registry of Friendly Societies 15/17 Great Marlborough Street London W1V 2AX *for Scottish Registered Companies* Assistant Registrar of Friendly Societies 58 Frederick Street Edinburgh EH2 1NB
Dentist, Dental Surgeon, Dental Practitioner	General Dental Council 37 Wimpole Street London W1M 8DQ
Drug, Druggist, Pharmaceutical, Pharmaceutist, Pharmacist, Pharmacy	The Royal Pharmaceutical Society of Great Britain Law Department 1 Lambeth High Street London SE1 7JN *for Scottish Registered Companies* The Pharmaceutical Society of Great Britain 36 York Place Edinburgh EH1 3HU
Insurance Broker, Assurance Broker, Re-Insurance Broker, Re-Assurance Broker	Insurance Brokers Registration Council 15 St. Helen's Place London EC3A 6DS
Olympiad, Olympiads, Olympian, Olympians, Olympic, Olympics	British Olympic Association 1 Wandsworth Plain London SW18 1EH

Word or Expression	Appropriate body
Optician, Ophthalmic Optician, Dispensing Optician, Enrolled Optician, Registered Optician, Optometrist	General Optical Council 41 Harley Street London W1N 2DJ
Patent Office, Patent Agent	IPCD Hazlitt House 45 Southampton Buildings London WC2A 1AR
Red Cross, Red Crescent, Geneva Cross	*Seek advice of Companies House*
Veterinary Surgeon, Veterinary, Vet	Royal College of Veterinary Surgeons 62–64 Horseferry Road London SW1P 2AF

The forms in this guide

The forms in this guide

The Companies Acts 1985 to 1989
Private Company Limited by Shares

MEMORANDUM OF ASSOCIATION OF
LIMITED

1. The company's name is " Limited".
2. The company's registered office is to be situated in England or Wales.
3. The objects of the company are to carry on business as a general commercial company and to do all such things as are incidental to the carrying on of any trade or business by it.
4. The liability of the members is limited.
5. The company's share capital is £100 divided into 100 shares of £1 each.

We, the subscribers to this Memorandum of Association, wish to be formed into a company pursuant to this Memorandum; and we agree to take the number of shares shown opposite our respective names.

Signatures, names and addresses of subscribers.

Number of shares taken by each subscriber.

1. Signature   _____
   Name   _____
   Address   _____   _____

2. Signature   _____
   Name   _____
   Address   _____   _____

Total shares taken _____   _____
     _____

Dated this _____ day of _____ year _____

Witness to the above signature Signature _____
                                Name _____
                              Address _____
                                          _____

The Companies Acts 1985 to 1989
Private Company Limited by Shares

MEMORANDUM OF ASSOCIATION OF
Law Pack Publishing   LIMITED

1. The company's name is " **Law Pack Publishing** Limited".

2. The company's registered office is to be situated in England or Wales.

3. The objects of the company are to carry on business as a general commercial company and to do all such things as are incidental to the carrying on of any trade or business by it.

4. The liability of the members is limited.

5. The company's share capital is £100 divided into 100 shares of £1 each.

We, the subscribers to this Memorandum of Association, wish to be formed into a company pursuant to this Memorandum; and we agree to take the number of shares shown opposite our respective names.

Signatures, names and addresses of subscribers.	Number of shares taken by each subscriber.

1. Signature   *A Palmer*
    Name   Alexander Palmer   one
    Address   85 Preston Square London SW6 5CN

2. Signature   *Julia Etheridge*
    Name   Julia Etheridge   one
    Address   16 St. George's Crescent Reading RG7 9XY

Total shares taken   two

Dated this ___3___ day of ___January___ year _1999_

Witness to the above signatures.   Signature   *Adam Bennett*
                                   Name   Adam Bennett
                                   Address   32 Church Grove
                                               London SW6 6RQ

The Companies Acts 1985 to 1989
Private Company Limited by Shares

MEMORANDUM OF ASSOCIATION OF
LIMITED

1. The company's name is "   Limited".

2. The company's registered office is to be situated in Scotland.

3. The objects of the company are to carry on business as a general commercial company and to do all such things as are incidental to the carrying on of any trade or business by it.

4. The liability of the members is limited.

5. The company's share capital is £100 divided into 100 shares of £1 each.

We, the subscribers to this Memorandum of Association, wish to be formed into a company pursuant to this Memorandum; and we agree to take the number of shares shown opposite our respective names.

Signatures, names and addresses of subscribers.

Number of shares taken by each subscriber.

1.   Signature   _____
   Name   _____
   Address   _____
   Occupation or Designation _____

2.   Signature   _____
   Name   _____
   Address   _____
   Occupation or Designation _____

Total shares taken

Dated this _____ day of _____ year ____

Witness to the above signatures.   Signature   _____
   Name   _____
   Address   _____

Occupation or Designation _____

The Companies Acts 1985 to 1989
Private Company Limited by Shares

MEMORANDUM OF ASSOCIATION OF
Law Pack Publishing   LIMITED

1. The company's name is "   **Law Pack Publishing**   Limited".

2. The company's registered office is to be situated in Scotland.

3. The objects of the company are to carry on business as a general commercial company and to do all such things as are incidental to the carrying on of any trade or business by it.

4. The liability of the members is limited.

5. The company's share capital is £100 divided into 100 shares of £1 each.

We, the subscribers to this Memorandum of Association, wish to be formed into a company pursuant to this Memorandum; and we agree to take the number of shares shown opposite our respective names.

Signatures, names and addresses of subscribers.

Number of shares taken by each subscriber.

1. Signature   *A Palmer*
    Name   Alexander Palmer
    Address   30 High Street Edinburgh EH1 2AB
    Occupation or Designation   Sales Manager

    one

2. Signature   *Julia Etheridge*
    Name   Julia Etheridge
    Address   30 East Street Glasgow G1 2BC
    Occupation or Designation   Office Manager

    one

Total shares taken

two

Dated this   3   day of   January   year   1999

Witness to the above signatures.   Signature   *Adam Bennett*
    Name   Adam Bennett
    Address   45 West Street
    Edinburgh EH2 3BC
    Occupation or Designation   Supervisor

The Companies Act 1985 to 1989
Private Company Limited by Shares

ARTICLES OF ASSOCIATION OF

LIMITED

INTERPRETATION

1. **In these articles –**

'the Act' means the Companies Act 1985 including any statutory modification or re-enactment thereof for the time being in force.

'the articles' means these articles.

'clear days' in relation to the period of a notice means that period excluding the day when the notice is given or deemed to be given and the day for which it is given or on which it is to take effect.

'executed' includes any mode of execution.

'office' means the registered office of the company.

'the holder' in relation to shares means the member whose name is entered in the register of members as the holder of the shares.

'the seal' means the common seal of the company.

'secretary' means the secretary of the company or any other person appointed to perform the duties of the secretary of the company, including a joint, assistant or deputy secretary.

'the United Kingdom' means Great Britain and Northern Ireland.

Unless the context otherwise requires, words or expressions contained in these articles bear the same meaning as in the Act but excluding any statutory modification thereof not in force when these articles become binding on the company.

SHARE CAPITAL

2. Subject to the provisions of the Act and without prejudice to any rights attached to any existing shares, any share may be issued with such rights or restrictions as the company may by ordinary resolution determine.

3. Subject to the provisions of the Act, shares may be issued which are to be redeemed or are to be liable to be redeemed at the option of the company or the holder on such terms and in such manner as may be provided by the articles.

4. The company may exercise the powers of paying commissions conferred by the Act. Subject to the provisions of the Act, any such commission may be satisfied by the payment of cash or by the allotment of fully or partly paid shares or partly in one way and partly in the other.

5. Except as required by law, no person shall be recognised by the company as holding any share upon any trust and (except as otherwise provided by the articles or by law) the company shall not be bound by or recognise any interest in any share except an absolute right to the entirety thereof in the holder.

6. The directors are generally and unconditionally authorised for the purposes of section 80 of the Companies Act 1985 to allot and grant rights to subscribe for or to convert securities into shares of the company to such persons at such times and generally on such terms and conditions as the directors may determine during the period commencing on the date of incorporation and expiring on the fifth anniversary thereof up to a maximum aggregate nominal amount of such shares of £10,100.

SHARE CERTIFICATES

7. Every member, upon becoming the holder of any shares, shall be entitled without payment to one certificate for all the shares of each class held by him (and, upon transferring a part of his holding of shares of any class, to a certificate for the balance of such holding) or several certificates each for one or more of his shares upon payment for every certificate after the first of such reasonable sum as the directors may determine. Every certificate shall be sealed with the seal and shall specify the number, class and distinguishing numbers (if any) of the shares to which it relates and the amount or respective amounts paid up thereon. The company shall not be bound to issue more than one certificate for shares held jointly by several persons and delivery of a certificate to one joint holder shall be a sufficient delivery to all of them.

8. If a share certificate is defaced, worn-out, lost or destroyed, it may be renewed on such terms (if any) as to evidence and indemnity and payment of the expenses reasonably incurred by the company in investigating evidence as the directors may determine but otherwise free of charge, and (in the case of defacement or wearing-out) on delivery up of the old certificate.

LIEN

9. The company shall have a first and paramount lien on every share (not being a fully paid share) for all moneys (whether presently payable or not) payable at a fixed time or called in respect of that share. The directors may at any time declare any share to be wholly or in part exempt from the provisions of this article. The company's lien on a share shall extend to any amount payable in respect of it.

10. The company may sell in such manner as the directors determine any shares on which the company has a lien if a sum in respect of which the lien exists is presently payable and is not paid within fourteen clear days after notice has been given to the holder of the share or to the person entitled to it in consequence of the death or bankruptcy of the holder, demanding payment and stating that if the notice is not complied with the shares may be sold.

11. To give effect to a sale the directors may authorise some person to execute an instrument of transfer of the shares sold to, or in accordance with the directions of, the purchaser. The title of the transferee to the shares shall not be affected by any irregularity in or invalidity of the proceedings in reference to the sale.

12. The net proceeds of the sale, after payment of the costs, shall be applied in payment of so much of the sum for which the lien exists as is presently payable, and any residue shall (upon surrender to the company for cancellation of the certificate for the shares sold and subject to a like lien for any moneys not presently payable as existed upon the shares before the sale) be paid to the person entitled to the shares at the date of the sale.

CALLS ON SHARES AND FORFEITURE

13. Subject to the terms of allotment, the directors may make calls upon the members in respect of any moneys unpaid on their shares (whether in respect of nominal value or premium) and each member shall (subject to receiving at least fourteen clear days' notice specifying when and where payment is to be made) pay to the company as required by the notice the amount called on his shares. A call may be required to be paid by instalments. A call may, before receipt by the company of any sum due thereunder, be revoked in whole or part and payment of a call may be postponed in whole or part. A person upon whom a call is made shall remain liable for calls made upon him notwithstanding the subsequent transfer of the shares in respect whereof the call was made.

14. A call shall be deemed to have been made at the time when the resolution of the directors authorising the call was passed.

15. The joint holders of a share shall be jointly and severally liable to pay all calls in respect thereof.

16. If a call remains unpaid after it has become due and payable the person from whom it is due and payable shall pay interest on the amount unpaid from the day it became due and payable until it is paid at the rate fixed by the terms of allotment of the share or in the notice of the call, or if no rate is fixed, at the appropriate rate (as defined by the Act) but the directors may waive payment of the interest wholly or in part.

17. An amount payable in respect of a share on allotment or at any fixed date, whether in respect of nominal value or premium or as an instalment of a call, shall be deemed to be a call and if not paid the provisions of the articles shall apply as if that amount had become due and payable by virtue of a call.

18. Subject to the terms of allotment, the directors may make arrangements on the issue of shares for a difference between the holders in the amounts and times of payment of calls on their shares.

19. If a call remains unpaid after it has become due and payable the directors may give to the person from whom it is due not less than fourteen clear days' notice requiring payment of the amount unpaid together with any interest which may have accrued. The notice shall name the place where payment is to be made and shall state that if the notice is not complied with the shares in respect of which the call was made will be liable to be forfeited.

20. If the notice is not complied with any share in respect of which it was given may, before the payment required by the notice has been made, be forfeited by a resolution of the directors and the forfeiture shall include all dividends or other moneys payable in respect of the forfeited shares and not paid before the forfeiture.

21. Subject to the provisions of the Act, a forfeited share may be sold, re-allotted or otherwise disposed of on such terms and in such manner as the directors determine either to the person who was before the forfeiture the holder or to any other person and at any time before sale, re-allotment or other disposition, the forfeiture may be cancelled on such terms as the directors think fit. Where for the purposes of its disposal a forfeited share is to be transferred to any person the directors may authorise some person to execute an instrument of transfer of the share to that person.

22. A person any of whose shares have been forfeited shall cease to be a member in respect of them and shall surrender to the company for cancellation the certificate for the shares forfeited but shall remain liable to the company for all moneys which at the date of forfeiture where presently payable by him to the company in respect of those shares with interest at the rate at which interest was payable on those moneys before the forfeiture or, if no interest was so payable, at the appropriate rate (as defined in the Act) from the date of forfeiture until payment but the directors may waive payment wholly or in part or enforce payment without any allowance for the value of the shares at the time of forfeiture or for any consideration received on their disposal.

23. A statutory declaration by a director or the secretary that a share has been forfeited on a specified date shall be conclusive evidence of the facts stated in it as against all persons claiming to be entitled to the share and the declaration shall (subject to the execution of an instrument of transfer if necessary) constitute a good title to the share and the person to whom the share is disposed of shall not be bound to see to the application of the consideration, if any, nor shall his title to the share be affected by any irregularity in or invalidity of the proceedings in reference to the forfeiture or disposal of the share.

TRANSFER OF SHARES

24. The instrument of transfer of a share may be in any usual form or in any other form which the directors may approve and shall be executed by or on behalf of the transferor and, unless the share is fully paid, by or on behalf of the transferee.

25. (a) (i) A person whether a member of the company or not ('the proposing transferor') proposing to transfer any shares shall give a notice in writing (a 'transfer notice') to the company that he desires to transfer such shares, and the transfer notice shall constitute the company his agent for the sale of all (but not a part only) of the shares specified in the notice to any member or members at the prescribed price (as defined below). A transfer notice once received by the company shall not be revocable without the prior consent of the directors;

(ii) if within a period of 28 days after receiving a transfer notice the company finds a member or members ('the purchaser') willing to purchase all the shares specified in the transfer notice the company shall give written notice of the fact to the proposing transferor and he shall be bound upon payment of the prescribed price to transfer those shares to the purchaser;

(iii) every notice given by the company under the preceding paragraph stating that it has found a purchaser for the shares specified in the transfer notice shall state the name and address of the purchaser and the number of shares which he has agreed to purchase. The purchase shall be completed at a place and time to be appointed by the company, not being more than 28 days after the prescribed price shall have been agreed or determined under paragraph 25 (a)(vi) of this article. For the purpose of determining the right to any distribution by the company, the proposing transferor shall be deemed to have sold such shares on the date of the notice so given by the company;

(iv) if the proposing transferor, after having become bound to transfer any shares to a purchaser, fails to do so, the directors may authorise some person to sign an instrument of transfer on behalf of the proposing transferor in favour of the purchaser, and the company may receive the purchase money, and shall at that time cause the name of the purchaser to be entered in the register as the holder of the shares and shall hold the purchase money in trust for the proposing transferor. The receipt of the company for the purchase money shall be a good discharge to the purchaser, who shall not be bound to see to its application; and after his name has been entered in the register the validity of the proceedings shall not be questioned by any person;

(v) if within a period of 28 days after receiving a transfer notice ('the prescribed period') the company shall not find purchasers for all the shares specified in the transfer notice, and gives notice in writing to that effect to the proposing transferor, or if the company within the prescribed period gives to the proposing transferor notice in writing that it has no prospect of finding such purchasers, the proposing transferor shall be at liberty, until the expiration of four months after the end of the prescribed period, to transfer all or any of the shares specified in the transfer notice to any person and at any price, or by way of gift; provided that, if the directors shall so resolve, the company may when giving notice under this paragraph inform the proposing transferor that the company will, subject to and in accordance with the provisions of chapter VII of part V of the Act, as soon as practicable purchase all the shares specified in the transfer notice at the prescribed price, and such notice shall be binding upon the company and the proposing transferor, who shall respectively take all steps within their power for carrying such purchase into effect;

    (vi) if within one month after the receipt by the proposing transferor of a notice given by the company under paragraph 25(a)(ii) of this article he shall have agreed with the purchaser a price per share for any shares then that price shall be the prescribed price of those shares. For any other shares, the auditors for the time being of the company or (if the proposing transferor shall so request) some other chartered accountant nominated by the President of the Institute of Chartered Accountants in England shall determine the fair value of such shares, the value so determined being the prescribed price for those shares and in determining the prescribed price they or he shall have power to determine how the costs of fixing it shall be borne. In making the determination the auditors or the chartered accountant nominated by the President of the Institute of Chartered Accountants shall act as an expert and not as an arbitrator and their or his determination shall be final and binding;

    (vii) all shares comprised in any transfer notice shall be offered by the company in the first instance for sale at the prescribed price to all members holding shares of the same class as those so comprised (other than the proposing transferor) on the terms that in case of competition the shares so offered shall be sold to the members accepting the offer in proportion (as nearly as may be) to their existing holdings of such shares. All offers of shares under this paragraph shall be made in writing and sent by prepaid post to the members at their respective registered addresses, and shall limit a time (not being less than 21 days) within which the offer must be accepted or in default will be treated as declined.

    (b) The directors may in their absolute discretion and without assigning any reason therefor decline to register any transfer of any share including any transfer which would otherwise be permitted under the preceding provisions of this article.

26. If the directors refuse to register a transfer of a share, they shall within two months after the date on which the transfer was lodged with the company send to the transferee notice of the refusal.

27. The registration of transfers of shares or of transfers of any class of shares may be suspended at such times and for such periods (not exceeding thirty days in any year) as the directors may determine.

28. No fee shall be charged for the registration of any instrument of transfer or other document relating to or affecting the title to any share.

29. The company shall be entitled to retain any instrument of transfer which is registered, but any instrument of transfer which the directors refuse to register shall be returned to the person lodging it when notice of the refusal is given.

TRANSMISSION OF SHARES

30. If a member dies the survivor or survivors where he was a joint holder, and his personal representatives where he was a sole holder or the only survivor of joint holders, shall be the only persons recognised by the company as having any title to his interest; but nothing herein contained shall release the estate of a deceased member from any liability in respect of any share which had been jointly held by him.

31. A person becoming entitled to a share in consequence of the death or bankruptcy of a member may, upon such evidence being produced as the directors may properly require, elect either to become the holder of the share or to have some person nominated by him registered as the transferee. If he elects to become the holder he shall give notice to the company to that effect. If he elects to have another person registered he shall execute an instrument of transfer of the share to that person. All the articles relating to the transfer of shares shall apply to the notice or instrument of transfer as if it were an instrument of transfer executed by the member and the death or bankruptcy of the member had not occurred.

32. A person becoming entitled to a share in consequence of the death or bankruptcy of a member shall have the rights to which he would be entitled if he were the holder of the share, except that he shall not, before being registered as the holder of the share, be entitled in respect of it to attend or vote at any meeting of the company or at any separate meeting of the holders of any class of shares in the company.

ALTERATION OF SHARE CAPITAL

33. The company may by ordinary resolution –

    (a) increase its share capital by new shares of such amount as the resolution prescribes;

    (b) consolidate and divide all or any of its share capital into shares of larger amount than its existing shares;

    (c) subject to the provision of the Act, sub-divide its shares, or any of them, into shares of smaller amounts and the resolution may determine that, as between the shares resulting from the sub-division, any of them may have any preference or advantage as compared with the others; and

    (d) cancel shares which, at the date of the passing of the resolution, have not been taken or agreed to be taken by any person and diminish the amount of its share capital by the amount of the shares so cancelled.

34. Whenever as a result of a consolidation of shares any members would become entitled to fractions of a share, the directors may, on behalf of those members, sell the shares representing the fractions for the best price reasonably obtainable to any person (including, subject to the provisions of the Act, the company) and distribute the net proceeds of sale in due proportion among those members, and the directors may authorise some person to execute an instrument of transfer of the shares to, or in accordance with the direction of, the purchaser. The transferee shall not be bound to see to the application of the purchase money nor shall his title to the shares be affected by any irregularity in or invalidity of the proceedings in reference to the sale.

35. Subject to the provisions of the Act, the company may by special resolution reduce its share capital, any capital redemption reserve and any share premium account in any way.

PURCHASE OF OWN SHARES

36. Subject to the provisions of the Act, the company may purchase its own shares (including any redeemable shares) and, if it is a private company, make a payment in respect of the redemption or purchase of its own shares otherwise than out of distributable profits of the company or the proceeds of a fresh issue of shares.

GENERAL MEETINGS

37. All general meetings other than annual general meetings shall be called extraordinary general meetings.

38. The directors may call general meetings and, on the requisition of members pursuant to the provisions of the Act, shall forthwith proceed to convene an extraordinary general meeting for a date not later than eight weeks after receipt of the requisition. If there are not within the United Kingdom sufficient directors to call a general meeting, any director or any member of the company may call a general meeting.

NOTICE OF GENERAL MEETINGS

39. An annual general meeting and an extraordinary general meeting called for the passing of a special resolution or a resolution appointing a person as a director shall be called by at least twenty-one clear days' notice. All other extraordinary general meetings shall be called by at least fourteen clear days' notice but a general meeting may be called by shorter notice if it is so agreed –

    (a) in the case of an annual general meeting, by all the members entitled to attend and vote thereat; and

    (b) in the case of any other meeting by a majority in number of the members having a right to attend and vote being a majority together holding not less than ninety-five per cent in nominal value of the shares giving that right.

The notice shall specify the time and place of the meeting and the general nature of the business to be transacted and, in the case of an annual general meeting, shall specify the meeting as such.

Subject to the provisions of the articles and to any restrictions imposed on any shares, the notice shall be given to all the members, to all persons entitled to a share in consequence of the death or bankruptcy of a member and to the directors and auditors.

40. The accidental omission to give notice of a meeting to, or the non-receipt of notice of a

meeting by, any person entitled to receive notice shall not invalidate the proceedings at that meeting.

PROCEEDINGS AT GENERAL MEETINGS

41. No business shall be transacted at any meeting unless a quorum is present. Two persons entitled to vote upon the business to be transacted, each being a member or a proxy for a member or a duly authorised representative of a corporation, shall be a quorum.

42. If such a quorum is not present within half an hour from the time appointed for the meeting, or if during a meeting such a quorum ceases to be present, the meeting shall stand adjourned to the same day in the next week at the same time and place or to such time and place as the directors may determine.

43. The chairman, if any, of the board of directors or in his absence some other director nominated by the directors shall preside as chairman of the meeting, but if neither the chairman nor such other director (if any) be present within fifteen minutes after the time appointed for holding the meeting and willing to act, the directors present shall elect one of their number to be chairman and, if there is only one director present and willing to act, he shall be chairman.

44. If no director is willing to act as chairman, or if no director is present within fifteen minutes after the time appointed for holding the meeting, the members present and entitled to vote shall choose one of their number to be chairman.

45. A director shall, notwithstanding that he is not a member, be entitled to attend and speak at any general meeting and at any separate meeting of the holders of any class of shares in the company.

46. The chairman may, with the consent of a meeting at which a quorum is present (and shall if so directed by the meeting), adjourn the meeting from time to time and from place to place, but no business shall be transacted at an adjourned meeting other than business which might properly have been transacted at the meeting had the adjournment not taken place. When a meeting is adjourned for fourteen days or more, at least seven clear days' notice shall be given specifying the time and place of the adjourned meeting and the general nature of the business to be transacted. Otherwise it shall not be necessary to give any such notice.

47. A resolution put to the vote of a meeting shall be decided on a show of hands unless before, or on the declaration of the result of, the show of hands a poll is duly demanded. Subject to the provisions of the Act, a poll may be demanded –

    (a) by the chairman; or

    (b) by at least two members having the right to vote at the meeting; or

    (c) by a member or members representing not less than one-tenth of the total voting rights of all the members having the right to vote at the meeting; or

    (d) by a member or members holding shares conferring a right to vote at the meeting being shares on which an aggregate sum has been paid up equal to not less than one-tenth of the total sum paid up on all the shares conferring that right;

and a demand by a person as proxy for a member shall be the same as a demand by the member.

48. Unless a poll is duly demanded a declaration by the chairman that a resolution has been carried or carried unanimously, or by a particular majority, or lost, or not carried by a particular majority and an entry to that effect in the minutes of the meeting shall be conclusive evidence of the fact without proof of the number or proportion of the votes recorded in favour of or against the resolution.

49. The demand for a poll may, before the poll is taken, be withdrawn but only with the consent of the chairman and a demand so withdrawn shall not be taken to have invalidated the result of a show of hands declared before the demand was made.

50. A poll shall be taken as the chairman directs and he may appoint scrutineers (who need not be members) and fix a time and place for declaring the result of the poll. The result of the poll shall be deemed to be the resolution of the meeting at which the poll was demanded.

51. In the case of an equality of votes, whether on a show of hands or on a poll, the chairman shall not be entitled to a casting vote in addition to any other vote he may have.

52. A poll demanded on the election of a chairman or on a question of adjournment shall be taken forthwith. A poll demanded on any other question shall be taken either forthwith or at such time and place as the chairman directs not being more than thirty days after the poll is demanded. The demand for a poll shall not prevent the continuance of a meeting for the transaction of any business other than the question on which the poll was demanded. If a poll is demanded before the declaration of the result of a show of hands and the demand is duly withdrawn, the meeting shall continue as if the demand had not been made.

53. No notice need be given of a poll not taken forthwith if the time and place at which it is to be taken are announced at the meeting at which it is demanded. In any other case at least seven clear days' notice shall be given specifying the time and place at which the poll is to be taken.

54. A resolution in writing executed by or on behalf of each member who would have been entitled to vote upon it if it had been proposed at a general meeting at which he was present shall be as effectual as if it had been passed at a general meeting duly convened and held and may consist of several instruments in the like form each executed by or on behalf of one or more members.

VOTES OF MEMBERS

55. Subject to any rights or restrictions attached to any shares, on a show of hands every member who (being an individual) is present in person or (being a corporation) is present by a duly authorised representative, not being himself a member entitled to vote, shall have one vote and on a poll every member shall have one vote for every share of which he is the holder.

56. In the case of joint holders the vote of the senior who tenders a vote, whether in person or by proxy, shall be accepted to the exclusion of the votes of the other joint holders; and seniority shall be determined by the order in which the names of the holders stand in the register of members.

57. A member in respect of whom an order has been made by any court having jurisdiction (whether in the United Kingdom or elsewhere) in matters concerning mental disorder may vote, whether on a show of hands or on a poll, by his receiver, curator bonis or other person authorised in that behalf appointed by that court, and any such receiver, curator bonis or other person may, on a poll, vote by proxy. Evidence to the satisfaction of the directors of the authority of the person claiming to exercise the right to vote shall be deposited at the office, or at such other place as is specified in accordance with the articles for the deposit of instruments of proxy, not less than 48 hours before the time appointed for holding the meeting or adjourned meeting at which the right to vote is to be exercised and in default the right to vote shall not be exercisable.

58. No member shall vote at any general meeting or at any separate meeting of the holders of any class of shares in the company, either in person or by proxy, in respect of any share held by him unless all moneys presently payable by him in respect of that share have been paid.

59. No objection shall be raised to the qualification of any voter except at the meeting or adjourned meeting at which the vote objected to is tendered, and every vote not disallowed at the meeting shall be valid. Any objection made in due time shall be referred to the chairman whose decision shall be final and conclusive.

60. On a poll votes may be given either personally or by proxy. A member may appoint more than one proxy to attend on the same occasion.

61. An instrument appointing a proxy shall be in writing, executed by or on behalf of the appointor and shall be in the following form (or in a form as near thereto as circumstances allow or in any other form which is usual or which the directors may approve) –

PLC/Limited

'I/We,   of   being a member/members of the above-named company, hereby appoint   of   , or failing him,   of   as my/our proxy to vote in my/our name(s) and on my/our behalf at the annual/extraordinary general meeting of the company to be held
on   year   , and at any adjournment thereof.
Signed   on   year   .'

62. Where it is desired to afford members an opportunity of instructing the proxy how he shall act the instrument appointing a proxy shall be in the following form (or in a form as near thereto as circumstances allow or in any other form which is usual or which the directors may approve) –

PLC/Limited

'I/We,   of   , being a member/members of the above-named company, hereby appoint   of   , or failing him,   of   , as my/our proxy to vote in my/our name(s) and on my/our behalf at the annual/extraordinary general meeting of the company, to be held on year , and at any adjournment thereof. This form is to be used in respect of the resolutions mentioned below as follows:

Resolution No. 1 *for *against

Resolution No. 2 *for *against

** Strike out whichever is not desired*

Unless otherwise instructed, the proxy may vote as he thinks fit or abstain from voting.

Signed this day of year .'

63. The instrument appointing a proxy and any authority under which it is executed or a copy of such authority certified notarially or in some other way approved by the directors may –

(a) be deposited at the office or at such other place within the United Kingdom as is specified in the notice convening the meeting or in any instrument of proxy sent out by the company in relation to the meeting not less than 48 hours before the time for holding the meeting or adjourned meeting at which the person named in the instrument proposes to vote; or

(b) in the case of a poll taken more than 48 hours after it is demanded, be deposited as aforesaid after the poll has been demanded and not less than 24 hours before the time appointed for the taking of the poll; or

(c) where the poll is not taken forthwith but is taken not more than 48 hours after it was demanded, be delivered at the meeting at which the poll was demanded to the chairman or to the secretary or to any director; and an instrument of proxy which is not deposited or delivered in a manner so permitted shall be invalid.

64. A vote given or poll demanded by proxy or by the duly authorised representative of a corporation shall be valid notwithstanding the previous determination of the authority of the person voting or demanding a poll unless notice of the determination was received by the company at the office or at such other place at which the instrument of proxy was duly deposited before the commencement of the meeting or adjourned meeting at which the vote is given or the poll demanded or (in the case of a poll taken otherwise than on the same day as the meeting or adjourned meeting) the time appointed for taking the poll.

NUMBER OF DIRECTORS

65. Unless otherwise determined by ordinary resolution, the number of directors (other than alternate directors) shall not be subject to any maximum but shall be not less than two.

ALTERNATE DIRECTORS

66. Any director (other than an alternate director) may appoint any other director, or any other person approved by resolution of the directors and willing to act, to be an alternate director and may remove from office an alternate director so appointed by him.

67. An alternate director shall be entitled to receive notice of all meetings of directors and of all meetings of committees of directors of which his appointor is a member, to attend and vote at any such meeting at which the director appointing him is not personally present, and generally to perform all the functions of his appointor as a director in his absence but shall not be entitled to receive any remuneration from the company for his services as an alternate director. But it shall not be necessary to give notice of such a meeting to an alternate director who is absent from the United Kingdom.

68. An alternate director shall cease to be an alternate director if his appointor ceases to be a director; but, if a director retires by rotation or otherwise but is reappointed or deemed to have been reappointed at the meeting at which he retires, any appointment of an alternate director made by him which was in force immediately prior to his retirement shall continue after his reappointment.

69. Any appointment or removal of an alternate director shall be by notice to the company signed by the director making or revoking the appointment or in any other manner approved by the directors.

70. Save as otherwise provided in the articles, an alternate director shall be deemed for all purposes to be a director and shall alone be responsible for his own acts and defaults and he shall not be deemed to be the agent of the director appointing him.

POWERS OF DIRECTORS

71. Subject to the provisions of the Act, the memorandum and the articles and to any directions given by special resolution, the business of the company shall be managed by the directors who may exercise all the powers of the company. No alteration of the memorandum or articles and no such direction shall invalidate any prior act of the directors which would have been valid if that alteration had not been made or that direction had not been given. The powers given by this article shall not be limited by any special power given to the directors by the articles and a meeting of directors at which a quorum is present may exercise all powers exercisable by the directors.

72. The directors may, by power of attorney or otherwise, appoint any person to be the agent of the company for such purposes and on such conditions as they determine, including authority for the agent to delegate all or any of his powers.

DELEGATION OF DIRECTORS' POWERS

73. The directors may delegate any of their powers to any committee consisting of one or more directors. They may also delegate to any managing director or any director holding any other executive office such of their powers as they consider desirable to be exercised by him. Any such delegation may be made subject to any conditions the directors may impose, and either collaterally with or to the exclusion of their own powers and may be revoked or altered. Subject to any such conditions, the proceedings of a committee with two or more members shall be governed by the articles regulating the proceedings of directors so far as they are capable of applying.

APPOINTMENT OF DIRECTORS

74. No person shall be appointed a director at any general meeting unless –

(a) he is recommended by the directors; or

(b) not less than fourteen nor more than thirty-five clear days before the date appointed for the meeting, notice executed by a member qualified to vote at the meeting has been given to the company of the intention to propose that person for appointment stating the particulars which would, if he were so appointed, be required to be included in the company's register of directors with notice executed by that person of his willingness to be appointed.

75. Not less than seven nor more than twenty-eight clear days before the date appointed for holding a general meeting notice shall be given to all who are entitled to receive notice of the meeting of any person who is recommended by the directors for appointment as a director at the meeting or in respect of whom notice has been duly given to the company of the intention to propose him at the meeting for appointment as a director. The notice shall give the particulars of the person which would, if he were so appointed, be required to be included in the company's register of directors.

76. Subject as aforesaid, the company may by ordinary resolution appoint a person who is willing to act to be a director either to fill a vacancy or as an additional director.

77. The directors may appoint a person who is willing to act to be a director, either to fill a vacancy or as an additional director, provided that the appointment does not cause the number of directors to exceed any number fixed by or in accordance with the articles as the maximum number of directors. A director so appointed shall hold office only until the next following annual general meeting. If not reappointed at such annual general meeting, he shall vacate office at the conclusion thereof.

DISQUALIFICATION AND REMOVAL OF DIRECTORS

78. The office of a director shall be vacated if –

(a) he ceases to be a director by virtue of any provision of the Act or he becomes prohibited by law from being a director; or

(b) he becomes bankrupt or makes any arrangement or composition with his creditors generally; or

(c) he is, or may be, suffering from mental disorder and either –

(i) he is admitted to hospital in pursuance of an application for admission for treatment under the Mental Health Act 1983 or, in Scotland, an application for admission under the Mental Health (Scotland) Act 1960, or

(ii) an order is made by a court having jurisdiction (whether in the United Kingdom or elsewhere) in matters concerning mental disorder for his detention or for the appointment of a receiver, curator bonis or other person to exercise powers with respect to his property or affairs; or

(d) he resigns his office by notice to the company; or

(e) he shall for more than six consecutive months have been absent without permission of the directors from meetings of directors held during that period and the directors resolve that his office be vacated.

REMUNERATION OF DIRECTORS

79. The directors shall be entitled to such remuneration as the company may by ordinary resolution determine and, unless the resolution provides otherwise, the remuneration shall be deemed to accrue from day to day.

DIRECTORS' EXPENSES

80. The directors may be paid all travelling, hotel, and other expenses properly incurred by them in connection with their attendance at meetings of directors or committees of directors or general meetings or separate meetings of the holders of any class of shares or of debentures of the company or otherwise in connection with the discharge of their duties.

DIRECTORS' APPOINTMENTS AND INTERESTS

81. Subject to the provisions of the Act, the directors may appoint one or more of their number to the office of managing director or to any other executive office under the company and may enter into an agreement or arrangement with any director for his employment by the company or for the provision by him of any services outside the scope of the ordinary duties of a director. Any such appointment, agreement or arrangement may be made upon such terms as the directors determine and they may remunerate any such director for his services as they think fit. Any appointment of a director to an executive office shall terminate if he ceases to be a director but without prejudice to any claim to damages for breach of the contract of service between the director and the company. A managing director and a director holding any other executive office shall not be subject to retirement by rotation.

82. Subject to the provisions of the Act, and provided that he has disclosed to the directors the nature and extent of any material interest of his, a director notwithstanding his office –

(a) may be a party to, or otherwise interested in, any transaction or arrangement with the company or in which the company is otherwise interested;

(b) may be a director or other officer of, or employed by, or a party to any transaction or arrangement with, or otherwise interested in, any body corporate promoted by the company or in which the company is otherwise interested; and

(c) shall not, by reason of his office, be accountable to the company for any benefit which he derives from any such office or employment or from any such transaction or arrangement or from any interest in any such body corporate and no such transaction or arrangement shall be liable to be avoided on the ground of any such interest or benefit.

83. For the purposes of article 82 –

(a) a general notice given to the directors that a director is to be regarded as having an interest of the nature and extent specified in the notice in any transaction or arrangement in which a specified person or class of persons is interested shall be deemed to be a disclosure that the director has an interest in any such transaction of the nature and extent so specified; and

(b) an interest of which a director has no knowledge and of which it is unreasonable to expect him to have knowledge shall not be treated as an interest of his.

DIRECTORS' GRATUITIES AND PENSIONS

84. The directors may provide benefits, whether by the payment of gratuities or pensions or by insurance or otherwise, for any director who has held but no longer holds any executive office or employment with the company or with any body corporate which is or has been a subsidiary of the company or a predecessor in business of the company or of any such subsidiary, and for any member of his family (including a spouse and a former spouse) or any person who is or was dependent on him, and may (as well before as after he ceases to hold such office or employment) contribute to any fund and pay premiums for the purchase or provision of any such benefit.

PROCEEDINGS OF DIRECTORS

85. Subject to the provisions of the articles, the directors may regulate their proceedings as they think fit. A director may, and the secretary at the request of a director shall, call a meeting of the directors. It shall not be necessary to give notice of a meeting to a director who is absent from the United Kingdom. Questions arising at a meeting shall be decided by a majority of votes. In the case of an equality of votes, the chairman shall not have a second or casting vote. A director who is also an alternate director shall be entitled in the absence of his appointor to a separate vote on behalf of his appointor in addition to his own vote.

86. The quorum for the transaction of the business of the directors may be fixed by the directors and unless so fixed at any other number shall be two. A person who holds office only as an alternate director shall, if his appointor is not present, be counted in the quorum.

87. The continuing directors or a sole continuing director may act notwithstanding any vacancies in their number, but, if the number of directors is less than the number fixed as the quorum, the continuing directors or director may act only for the purpose of filling vacancies or of calling a general meeting.

88. The directors may appoint one of the their number to be the chairman of the board of directors and may at any time remove him from that office. Unless he is unwilling to do so, the director so appointed shall preside at every meeting of directors at which he is present. But if there is no director holding that office, or if the director holding it is unwilling to preside or is not present within five minutes after the time appointed for the meeting, the directors present may appoint one of their number to be chairman of the meeting.

89. All acts done by a meeting of directors, or of a committee of directors, or by a person acting as a director shall, notwithstanding that it be afterwards discovered that there was a defect in the appointment of any director or that any of them were disqualified from holding office, or had vacated office, or were not entitled to vote, be as valid as if every such person has been duly appointed and was qualified and had continued to be a director and had been entitled to vote.

90. A resolution in writing signed by all the directors entitled to receive notice of a meeting of directors or of a committee of directors shall be as valid and effectual as if it had been passed at a meeting of directors or (as the case may be) a committee of directors duly convened and held and may consist of several documents in the like form each signed by one or more directors; but a resolution signed by an alternate director need not also be signed by his appointor and, if it is signed by a director who has appointed an alternate director, it need not be signed by the alternate director in that capacity.

91. Save as otherwise provided by the articles, a director shall not vote at a meeting of directors or of a committee of directors on any resolution concerning a matter in which he has, directly or indirectly, an interest or duty which is material and which conflicts or may conflict with the interests of the company unless his interest or duty arises only because the case falls within one or more of the following paragraphs –

(a) the resolution relates to the giving to him of a guarantee, security, or indemnity in respect of money lent to, or an obligation incurred by him for the benefit of, the company or any of its subsidiaries;

(b) the resolution relates to the giving to a third party of a guarantee, security, or indemnity in respect of an obligation of the company or any of its subsidiaries for which the director has assumed responsibility in whole or part and whether alone or jointly with others under a guarantee or indemnity or by the giving of security;

(c) his interest arises by virtue of his subscribing or agreeing to subscribe for any shares, debentures or other securities of the company or any of its subsidiaries, or by virtue of his being, or intending to become, a participant in the underwriting or sub-underwriting of an offer of any such shares, debentures, or other securities by the company or any of its subsidiaries for subscription, purchase or exchange;

(d) the resolution relates in any way to a retirement benefits scheme which has been approved, or is conditional upon approval, by the Board of Inland Revenue for taxation purposes.

For the purposes of this article, an interest of a person who is, for any purpose of the Act (excluding any statutory modification thereof not in force when this article becomes binding on the company), connected with a director shall be treated as an interest of the director and, in relation to an alternate director, an interest of his appointor shall be treated as an interest of the alternate director without prejudice to any interest which the alternate director has otherwise.

92. A director shall be counted in the quorum present at a meeting notwithstanding that at the meeting he is not entitled to vote on a resolution.

93. The company may by ordinary resolution suspend or relax to any extent, either generally or in respect of any particular matter, any provision of the articles prohibiting a director from voting at a meeting of directors or of a committee of directors.

94. Where proposals are under consideration concerning the appointment of two or more directors to offices or employments with the company or any body corporate in which the company is interested the proposals may be divided and considered in relation to each director separately and (provided he is not for another reason precluded from voting) each of the directors concerned shall be entitled to vote and be counted in the quorum in respect of each resolution except that concerning his own appointment.

95. If a question arises at a meeting of directors or of a committee of directors as to the right of a director to vote, the question may, before the conclusion of the meeting, be referred to the chairman of the meeting and his ruling in relation to any director other than himself shall be final and conclusive.

SECRETARY

96. Subject to the provisions of the Act, the secretary shall be appointed by the directors for such term, at such remuneration and upon such conditions as they may think fit; and any secretary so appointed may be removed by them.

MINUTES

97. The directors shall cause minutes to be made in books kept for the purpose –

(a) of all appointments of officers made by the directors; and

(b) of all proceedings at meetings of the company, of the holders of any class of shares in the company, and of the directors, and of committees of directors, including the names of the directors present at each such meeting.

THE SEAL

98. The seal shall only be used by the authority of the directors or of a committee of directors authorised by the directors. The directors may determine who shall sign any instrument to which the seal is affixed and unless otherwise so determined it shall be signed by a director and by the secretary or by a second director.

DIVIDENDS

99. Subject to the provisions of the Act, the company may by ordinary resolution declare dividends in accordance with the respective rights of the members, but no dividend shall exceed the amount recommended by the directors.

100. Subject to the provisions of the Act, the directors may pay interim dividends if it appears to them that they are justified by the profits of the company available for distribution. If the share capital is divided into different classes, the directors may pay interim dividends on shares which confer deferred or non-preferred rights with regard to dividend as well as on shares which confer preferential rights with regard to dividend, but no interim dividend shall be paid on shares carrying deferred or non-preferred rights if, at the time of payment, any preferential dividend is in arrear. The directors may also pay at intervals settled by them any dividend payable at a fixed rate if it appears to them that the profits available for distribution justify the payment. Provided the directors act in good faith they shall not incur any liability to the holders of shares conferring preferred rights for any loss they may suffer by the lawful payment of an interim dividend on any shares having deferred on non-preferred rights.

101. Except as otherwise provided by the rights attached to shares, all dividends shall be declared and paid according to the amounts paid up on the shares on which the dividend is paid. All dividends shall be apportioned and paid proportionately to the amounts paid up on the shares during any portion or portions of the period in respect of which the dividend is paid; but, if any share is issued on terms providing that it shall rank for dividend as from a particular date, that share shall rank for dividend accordingly.

102. A general meeting declaring a dividend may, upon the recommendation of the directors, direct that it shall be satisfied wholly or partly by the distribution of assets and, where any difficulty arises in regard to the distribution, the directors may settle the same and in particular may issue fractional certificates and fix the value for distribution of any assets and may determine that cash shall be paid to any member upon the footing of the value so fixed in order to adjust the rights of members and may vest any assets in trustees.

103. Any dividend or other moneys payable in respect of a share may be paid by cheque sent by post to the registered address of the person entitled or, if two or more persons are the holders of the share or are jointly entitled to it by reason of the death or bankruptcy of the holder, to the registered address of that one of those persons who is first named in the register of members or to such person and to such address as the person or persons entitled may in writing direct. Every cheque shall be made payable to the order of the person or persons entitled or to such other person as the person or persons entitled may in writing direct and payment of the cheque shall be a good discharge to the company. Any joint holder or other person jointly entitled to a share as aforesaid may give receipts for any dividend or other moneys payable in respect of the share.

104. No dividend or other moneys payable in respect of a share shall bear interest against the company unless otherwise provided by the rights attached to the share.

105. Any dividend which has remained unclaimed for twelve years from the date when it became due for payment shall, if the directors so resolve, be forfeited and cease to remain owing by the company.

ACCOUNTS

106. No member shall (as such) have any right of inspecting any accounting records or other book or document of the company except as conferred by statute or authorised by the directors or by ordinary resolution of the company.

CAPITALISATION OF PROFITS

107. The directors may with the authority of an ordinary resolution of the company –

(a) subject as hereinafter provided, resolve to capitalise any undivided profits of the company not required for paying any preferential dividend (whether or not they are available for distribution) or any sum standing to the credit of the company's share premium account or capital redemption reserve;

(b) appropriate the sum resolved to be capitalised to the members who would have been entitled to it if it were distributed by way of dividend and in the same proportions and apply such sum on their behalf either in or towards paying up the amounts, if any, for the time being unpaid on any shares held by them respectively, or in paying up in full unissued shares or debentures of the company of a nominal amount equal to that sum, and allot the shares or debentures credited as fully paid to those members, or as they may direct, in those proportions, or partly in one way and partly in the other: but the share premium account, the capital redemption reserve, and any profits which are not available for distribution may, for the purposes of this article, only be applied in paying up unissued shares to be allotted to members credited as fully paid;

(c) make such provision by the issue of fractional certificates or by payment in cash or otherwise as they determine in the case of shares or debentures becoming distributable under this article in fractions; and

(d) authorise any person to enter on behalf of all the members concerned into an agreement with the company providing for the allotment to them respectively, credited as fully paid, of any shares or debentures to which they are entitled upon such capitalisation, any agreement made under such authority being binding on all such members.

NOTICES

108. Any notice to be given to or by any person pursuant to the articles shall be in writing except that a notice calling a meeting of the directors need not be in writing.

109. The company may give any notice to a member either personally or by sending it by post in a prepaid envelope addressed to the member at his registered address or by leaving it at that address. In the case of joint holders of a share, all notices shall be given to the joint holder whose name stands first in the register of members in respect of the joint holding and notice so given shall be sufficient notice to all the joint holders. A member whose registered address is not within the United Kingdom and who gives to the company an address within the United Kingdom at which notices may be given to him shall be entitled to have notices given to him at that address, but otherwise no such member shall be entitled to receive any notice from the company.

110. A member present, either in person or by proxy, at any meeting of the company or of the holders of any class of shares in the company shall be deemed to have received notice of the meeting and, where requisite, of the purposes for which it was called.

111. Every person who becomes entitled to a share shall be bound by any notice in respect of that share which, before his name is entered in the register of members, has been duly given to a person from whom he derives his title.

112. Proof that an envelope containing a notice was properly addressed, prepaid and posted shall be conclusive evidence that the notice was given. A notice shall, unless the contrary is proved, be deemed to be given at the expiration of 48 hours after the envelope containing it was posted.

113. A notice may be given by the company to the persons entitled to a share in consequence of the death or bankruptcy of a member by sending or delivering it, in any manner authorised by the articles for the giving of notice to a member, addressed to them by name, or by the title of representatives of the deceased, or trustee of the bankrupt or by any like description at the address, if any, within the United Kingdom supplied for that purpose by the persons claiming to be so entitled. Until such an address has been supplied, a notice may be given in any manner in which it might have been given if the death or bankruptcy had not occurred.

WINDING UP

114. If the company is wound up, the liquidator may, with the sanction of an extraordinary resolution of the company and any other sanction required by the Act, divide among the members in specie the whole or any part of the assets of the company and may, for that purpose, value any assets and determine how the division shall be carried out as between the members or different classes of members. The liquidator may, with the like sanction, vest the whole or any part of the assets in trustees upon such trusts for the benefit of the members as he with the like sanction determines, but no member shall be compelled to accept any assets upon which there is a liability.

INDEMNITY

115. Subject to the provisions of the Act but without prejudice to any indemnity to which a director may otherwise be entitled, every director or other officer or auditor of the company shall be indemnified out of the assets of the company against any liability incurred by him in defending any proceedings, whether civil or criminal, in which judgment is given in his favour or in which he is acquitted or in connection with any application in which relief is granted to him by the court from liability for negligence, default, breach of duty or breach of trust in relation to the affairs of the company.

Signatures, names and addresses of subscribers.

1. Signature _____

    Name _____

    Address _____

    _____

Witness to the above signatures.

2. Signature _____   Signature _____

    Name _____   Name _____

    Address _____   Address _____

    _____   _____

Dated this _____ day of _____ year _____

Certificate No. _____

Number of Shares _____

LIMITED

𝕿𝖍𝖎𝖘 𝖎𝖘 𝖙𝖔 𝕮𝖊𝖗𝖙𝖎𝖋𝖞 that _____

of _____

is/are the Registered holder(s) of _____ shares of £ _____ each _____ paid

in the above-named Company, subject to the Memorandum and Articles of Association of the Company.

* This document is hereby executed by the Company /

The Common Seal of the Company was hereto affixed in the presence of:

_____

_____ Directors

_____ Secretary

_____ year

* *Delete as appropriate*

Certificate No. **1**   Number of Shares **1**

Law Pack Publishing   LIMITED

𝕿𝖍𝖎𝖘 𝖎𝖘 𝖙𝖔 𝕮𝖊𝖗𝖙𝖎𝖋𝖞 that   **Alexander Palmer**

of   **85 Preston Square, London SW6 5CN**

is/are the Registered holder(s) of   **1**   shares of £   **1**   each   **fully**   paid
in the above-named Company, subject to the Memorandum and Articles of Association of the Company.

* This document is hereby executed by the Company /
~~The Common Seal of the Company was hereto affixed in the presence of:~~

Julia Etheridge

Julia Etheridge   Directors

APalmer

Alexander Palmer   Secretary   **11th January**   year **1999**

* Delete as appropriate

Certificate No. **2**   Number of Shares **1**

Law Pack Publishing   LIMITED

𝕿𝖍𝖎𝖘 𝖎𝖘 𝖙𝖔 𝕮𝖊𝖗𝖙𝖎𝖋𝖞 that   **Julia Etheridge**

of   **16 St. George's Crescent, Reading RG7 9XY**

is/are the Registered holder(s) of   **1**   shares of £   **1**   each   **fully**   paid
in the above-named Company, subject to the Memorandum and Articles of Association of the Company.

* This document is hereby executed by the Company /
~~The Common Seal of the Company was hereto affixed in the presence of:~~

Julia Etheridge

Julia Etheridge   Directors

APalmer

Alexander Palmer   Secretary   **11th January**   year **1999**

* Delete as appropriate

10

First directors and secretary and intended situation of registered office

Please complete in typescript,
or in bold black capitals.
CHFP037

Notes on completion appear on final page

Company Name in full	Law Pack Publishing Limited

Proposed Registered Office	1 James Road
(PO Box numbers only, are not acceptable)	
Post town	**London**
County / Region		Postcode	**EC1 7OP**

If the memorandum is delivered by an agent for the subscriber(s) of the memorandum mark the box opposite and give the agent's name and address.

Agent's Name	**N/A**
Address	
Post town	
County / Region		Postcode	

Number of continuation sheets attached

Please give the name, address, telephone number and, if available, a DX number and Exchange of the person Companies House should contact if there is any query.

Alexander Palmer

Law Pack Publishing Limited, 1 James Road

London EC1 7OP Tel **0171-123 4567 Ext.890**

DX number   DX exchange

Companies House receipt date barcode

When you have completed and signed the form please send it to the Registrar of Companies at:
Companies House, Crown Way, Cardiff, CF4 3UZ   DX 33050 Cardiff
for companies registered in England and Wales
or
Companies House, 37 Castle Terrace, Edinburgh, EH1 2EB
for companies registered in Scotland   **DX 235 Edinburgh**

Form revised July 1998

Company Secretary (see notes 1-5)

Company name		Law Pack Publishing Ltd

NAME   *Style / Title   **Mr**   *Honours etc

* Voluntary details

Forename(s)   **Alexander**

Surname   **Palmer**

Previous forename(s)

Previous surname(s)

Address   **85 Preston Square**

Usual residential address
For a corporation, give the registered or principal office address.

London

Post town

County / Region   Postcode   **SW6 5CN**

Country

I consent to act as secretary of the company named on page 1

Consent signature   *APalmer*   **Date**   **3-1-99**

Directors (see notes 1-5)

Please list directors in alphabetical order

NAME   *Style / Title   *Honours etc

Forename(s)   **Mr**

Surname   **Alexander**

Previous forename(s)   **Palmer**

Previous surname(s)

Address   **85 Preston Square**

Usual residential address
For a corporation, give the registered or principal office address.

London

Post town

County / Region   Postcode   **SW6 5CN**

Country

	Day	Month	Year		
Date of birth	0 3	0 2	1 9 5 5	**Nationality**	**British**

Business occupation   **Company Director**

Other directorships   **None**

I consent to act as director of the company named on page 1

Consent signature   *APalmer*   **Date**   **3-1-99**

Directors (continued)   (see notes 1-5)

NAME	*Style / Title	Ms.	*Honours etc	

* Voluntary details

	Forename(s)	Julia

	Surname	Etheridge

	Previous forename(s)	

	Previous surname(s)	

Address

Usual residential address
For a corporation, give the registered or principal office address.

		16 St. George's Crescent

		Reading

	Post town	

	County / Region		Postcode	RG7 9XY

	Country	

	Day	Month	Year	
Date of birth	2 9	0 9	1 9 5 7	Nationality **British**

Business occupation	Sales Executive

Other directorships	Additional Co. Ltd.

I consent to act as director of the company named on page 1

Consent signature	*Julia Etheridge*	Date	3-1-99

This section must be signed by
Either

an agent on behalf of all subscribers

Signed		Date	

Or **the subscribers**

(i.e those who signed as members on the memorandum of association).

Signed	*APalmer*	Date	3-1-99
Signed	*Julia Etheridge*	Date	3-1-99
Signed		Date	
Signed		Date	
Signed		Date	
Signed		Date	

Notes

1. Show for an individual the full forename(s) NOT INITIALS and surname together with any previous forename(s) or surname(s).

   If the director or secretary is a corporation or Scottish firm - show the corporate or firm name on the surname line.

   Give previous forename(s) or surname(s) except that:

   - for a married woman, the name by which she was known before marriage need not be given,

   - names not used since the age of 18 or for at least 20 years need not be given.

   A peer, or an individual known by a title, may state the title instead of or in addition to the forename(s) and surname and need not give the name by which that person was known before he or she adopted the title or succeeded to it.

   Address:

   Give the usual residential address.

   In the case of a corporation or Scottish firm give the registered or principal office.

   Subscribers:

   The form must be signed personally either by the subscriber(s) or by a person or persons authorised to sign on behalf of the subscriber(s).

2. Directors known by another description:

   - A director includes any person who occupies that position even if called by a different name, for example, governor, member of council.

3. Directors details:

   - Show for each individual director the director's date of birth, business occupation and nationality. **The date of birth must be given for every individual director.**

4. Other directorships:

   - Give the name of every company of which the person concerned is a director or has been a director at any time in the past 5 years. You may exclude a company which either **is** or at **all times during the past 5 years,** when the person was a director, **was:**

   - dormant,

   - a parent company which wholly owned the company making the return,

   - a wholly owned subsidiary of the company making the return, or

   - another wholly owned subsidiary of the same parent company.

   If there is insufficient space on the form for other directorships you may use a separate sheet of paper, which should include the company's number and the full name of the director.

5. Use Form 10 continuation sheets or photocopies of page 2 to provide details of joint secretaries or additional directors.

12

Declaration on application for registration

Please complete in typescript,
or in bold black capitals.

CHFP037

Law Pack Publishing Limited

Company Name in full

I, | Alexander Palmer

of | 85 Preston Square London SW6 5CN

† *Please delete as appropriate.*

do solemnly and sincerely declare that I am a † [Solicitor engaged in the formation of the company][person named as director or secretary of the company in the statement delivered to the Registrar under section 10 of the Companies Act 1985] and that all the requirements of the Companies Act 1985 in respect of the registration of the above company and of matters precedent and incidental to it have been complied with.

And I make this solemn Declaration conscientiously believing the same to be true and by virtue of the Statutory Declarations Act 1835.

Declarant's signature | *A Palmer*

Declared at | 4 Richton Way Exeter EX1 2DN

| Day | Month | Year |
| 0 3 | 0 1 | 1 9 9 9 |

On

❶ *Please print name.*

before me ❶ | **Campbell Bush**

Signed | *Campbell Bush* | **Date** | 3/1/99

† A Commissioner for Oaths or Notary Public or Justice of the Peace or Solicitor

Please give the name, address, telephone number and, if available, a DX number and Exchange of the person Companies House should contact if there is any query.

Alexander Palmer

Law Pack Publishing Limited, 1 James Road

London EC1 7OP | Tel | **0171 123 4567**

DX number | DX exchange

Companies House receipt date barcode

When you have completed and signed the form please send it to the Registrar of Companies at:
Companies House, Crown Way, Cardiff, CF4 3UZ   **DX 33050 Cardiff**
for companies registered in England and Wales
or
Companies House, 37 Castle Terrace, Edinburgh, EH1 2EB
for companies registered in Scotland   **DX 235 Edinburgh**

Form revised June 1998

G

CHFP037

COMPANIES FORM No. 88(2)

Return of allotments of shares

88(2)

Pursuant to section 88(2) of the Companies Act 1985 (the Act)

Please do not write in this margin

Please complete legibly, preferably in black type, or bold block lettering

* insert full name of company

† distinguish between ordinary preference, etc.

§ complete (a) or (b) as appropriate

To the Registrar of Companies (**address overleaf**)
(see note 1)

(REVISED 1988)

This form replaces forms PUC2, PUC3 and 88(2)

Company number

| 1 2 3 4 5 6 7 |

1. Name of company

*	**Law Pack Publishing Limited**

2. This section must be completed for all allotments

Description of shares †	**Ordinary**		
A Number allotted	**2**		
B Nominal value of each	£ **1**	£	£
C Total amount (if any) paid or due and payable on each share (including premium if any)	£ **1**	£	£

Date(s) on which the shares were allotted
(a) [on **11th January   1999** ⅺ §, ⅺr
(b) [from _____ to _____] §
The names and addresses of the allottees and the number of shares allotted to each should be given overleaf

3. If the allotment is wholly or partly other than for cash the following information must be given **(see notes 2 & 3)**

D Extent to which each share is to be treated as paid up. Please use percentage	**N/A**		
E Consideration for which the shares were allotted	**N/A**		

NOTES
1. This form should be delivered to the Registrar of Companies within one month of the (first) date of allotment.
2. If the allotment is wholly or partly other than for cash, the company must deliver to the registrar a return containing the information at D & E. The company may deliver this information by completing D & E and the delivery of the information must be accompanied by the duly stamped contract required by section 88(2)(b) of the Act or by the duly stamped prescribed particulars required by section 88(3) (Form No 88(3)).
3. Details of bonus issues should be included only in section 2.

Presentor's name address and reference (if any) :

**Alexander Palmer
Law Pack Publishing
Limited
1 James Road
London EC1 7OP
0171 123 4567**

For official Use	Post room

Page 1

4. Names and addresses of the allottees

Names and Addresses	Number of shares allotted		
	Ordinary	Preference	Other
Alexander Palmer			
85 Preston Square			
London SW6	1		
Julia Etheridge			
16 St. George's Crescent			
Reading RG7 9XY	1		
Total	2		

Where the space given on this form is inadequate, continuation sheets should be used and the number of sheets attached should be indicated in the box opposite:

‡ Insert Director, Secretary, Administrator, Administrative Receiver or Receiver (Scotland) as appropriate

Signed *A Palmer* Designation **Director** Date **2-6-99**

Companies registered in England and Wales or Wales should deliver this form to:-

The Registrar of Companies
Companies House
Crown Way
Cardiff
CF4 3UZ

Companies registered in Scotland should deliver this form to:-

The Registrar of Companies
Companies House
37 Castle Terrace
Edinburgh
EH1 2EB

Page 2

COMPANIES FORM No. 123

Notice of increase in nominal capital

123

Please do not write in this margin

Pursuant to section 123 of the Companies Act 1985

Please complete legibly, preferably in black type, or bold block lettering

To the Registrar of Companies
(Address overleaf)

For official use

Company number

1234567

Name of company

* insert full name of company

*   **Law Pack Publishing Limited**

gives notice in accordance with section 123 of the above Act that by resolution of the company

dated _____**11th January 1999**_____the nominal capital of the company has been

increased by £ _____**900**_____ beyond the registered capital of £ _____**100**_____.

§ the copy must be printed or in some other form approved by the registrar

A copy of the resolution authorising the increase is attached.§

The conditions (eg. voting rights, dividend rights, winding-up rights etc.) subject to which the new

shares have been or are to be issued are as follow:

Please see Articles of Association of the company.

Please tick here if continued overleaf

‡ Insert Director, Secretary, Administrator, Administrative Receiver or Receiver (Scotland) as appropriate

Signed *A Palmer*   Designation‡ **Director**   Date **11-1-99**

Presentor's name address and reference (if any):

**Alexander Palmer
Law Pack Publishing
Limited
1 James Road
London EC1 7OP**

For official Use
General Section

Post room

225

Change of accounting reference date

Please complete in typescript,
or in bold black capitals
CHFP037

Company Number | 1234567

Company Name in Full | Law Pack Publishing Limited

NOTES

You may use this form to change the accounting date relating to either the current or the immediately previous accounting period.

a. You **may not** change a period for which the accounts are already overdue.

b. You **may not** extend a period beyond 18 months unless the company is subject to an administration order.

c. You **may not** extend periods more than once in five years unless:

   1. the company is subject to an administration order, or

   2. you have the specific approval of the Secretary of State, (please enclose a copy), or

   3. you are extending the company's accounting reference period to align with that of a parent or subsidiary undertaking established in the European Economic Area, or

   4. the form is being submitted by an oversea company.

The accounting reference period ending

Day	Month	Year
3 1	0 1	2 0 0 1

is shortened/extended† so as to end on

Day	Month	Year
3 1	1 2	2 0 0 0

Subsequent periods will end on the same day and month in future years.

If extending more than once in five years, please indicate in the box the number of the provision listed in note c. on which you are relying.

Signed | *APalmer* | **Date** | 11th January 1999

† Please delete as appropriate

† a director / secretary / administrator / administrative receiver / receiver and manager / receiver (Scotland) / person authorised on behalf of an oversea company

Please give the name, address, telephone number, and if available, a DX number and Exchange, for the person Companies House should contact if there is any query

Law Pack Publishing Limited

1 James Road

London EC1 7OP Tel **0171 123 4567**

DX number | DX exchange

Companies House receipt date barcode

When you have completed and signed the form please send it to the Registrar of Companies at:

Companies House, Crown Way, Cardiff, CF4 3UZ **DX 33050 Cardiff**

for companies registered in England and Wales

or

Companies House, 37 Castle Terrace, Edinburgh, EH1 2EB

for companies registered in Scotland **DX 235 Edinburgh**

Form revised July 1998

LAW PACK PUBLISHING LIMITED

Minutes of the first Meeting of the Directors held at 1 James Road, London EC1 on 11th January 1999 at 11 a.m.

PRESENT: **Alexander Palmer**   (In the Chair)
               Julia Etheridge

1.   The Chairman announced that a quorum was present and declared the Meeting open.

2.   There were produced to the Meeting the following:

    2.1   the Certificate of Incorporation of the Company (under No. 1234567) dated 9th January 1999;

    2.2   a copy of the Memorandum and Articles of Association of the Company as registered;

    2.3   a copy of Form 10, the statement required under section 10(2) Companies Act 1985 signed by the subscribers to the Memorandum of Association containing:

    (i)   particulars of the first Directors of the Company and the first Secretary of the Company and their respective consents to act in the relevant capacity; and

    (ii)   particulars of the intended situation of the registered office of the Company.

3.   IT WAS RESOLVED that:

    3.1   Alexander Palmer and Julia Etheridge each having subscribed to the Memorandum and Articles of Association for one ordinary share of £1 each, one such share be allotted and issued to each of them and certificates be issued in respect of such shares;

    3.2   Mr Palmer be and he is hereby appointed Chairman of the Directors;

    3.3   the register of Directors' interests in shares or debentures of the Company be kept at the registered office of the Company;

    3.4   a bank account for the Company be opened with National Bank plc, in accordance with the mandate lodged with the Bank;

    3.5   Messrs. Maxwells of 10 North Court, Manchester, Chartered Accountants, be and they are hereby appointed Auditors of the Company and their remuneration shall be agreed by the Board;

    3.6   the second accounting reference period of the Company be changed so as to be from 31st January 2000 to 31st December 2000 and consequently 31st December shall be the date on which in each successive calendar year an accounting reference period of the Company is to be treated as coming to an end;

    3.7   the Secretary be instructed to arrange for the filing with the Registrar of Companies all necessary returns, including:

    (i)   Form G88(2) (Return of allotments of shares);

    (ii)   Form 225 (Change of accounting reference date).

There being no further business the Meeting was closed.

A. Palmer

_____
Chairman

LAW PACK PUBLISHING LIMITED

Resolution of all the Directors in Office
Pursuant to Article 93 of the Company's Articles of Association dated 3rd January 1999

The Directors hereby confirm that they have before them the following:
1. The Certificate of Incorporation of the Company (under 1234567) dated 9th January 1999.
2. A copy of the Memorandum and Articles of Association of the Company as registered.
3. A copy of Form 10, the statement required under section 10 (2) Companies Act 1985 signed by the subscriber to the Memorandum of Association containing:
    i) Particulars of the first Directors of the Company and the first secretary of the Company and their respective consent to act in the relevant capacity;
    ii) Particulars of the intended situation of the registered office of the Company.

IT WAS RESOLVED that:
1. Alexander Palmer and Julia Etheridge having subscribed to the Memorandum and Articles of Association for one ordinary share of £1 each, one share be allotted and issued to each of them and Certificates be issued in respect of such shares.
2. The register of the Director's interests in shares or debentures of the Company be kept at the registered office of the Company.
3. A bank account for the Company be opened with National Bank plc in accordance with the mandate lodged with the bank.
4. Messrs. Maxwells of 10 North Court, Manchester, Chartered Accountants be and they are hereby appointed Auditors of the Company and their remuneration shall be agreed by us as Directors;
5. The second accounting reference period of the Company be changed so as to be from the 31st January 2000 to 31st December 2000 and consequently 31st December shall be the date on which in each successive calendar year an accounting reference period of the Company is to be treated as coming to an end;
6. The Secretary be instructed to arrange for the filing with the Registrar of Companies of all necessary returns including:
    i) Form G88(2) (Return of allotments of shares);
    ii) Form 225 (Change of accounting reference date).

A Palmer
_____
Director

Julia Etheridge
_____
Director

Register of   Members

Name   Alexander Palmer
Address   85 Preston Square
London SW6 5CN
Date of entry as shareholder   4-1-99   Date of cessation of membership _____

Date of Allotment OR Entry of Transfer	References in Register		Number of shares	No. of Share Certificate	Amount paid or agreed to be considered as paid	Acquisitions
	Allotments	Transfers				
11-1-99	✓		1	1	£1	

Dividends to   Alexander Palmer

Class of Share   Ordinary   **Denomination**   £1 each

Disposals	Balance	Remarks
	£1	

Name   Julia Etheridge
Address   16 St. George's Crescent
Reading RG7 9XY
Date of entry as shareholder   4-1-99   Date of cessation of membership _____

Date of Allotment OR Entry of Transfer	References in Register		Number of shares	No. of Share Certificate	Amount paid or agreed to be considered as paid	Acquisitions
	Allotments	Transfers				
11-1-99	✓		1	2	£1	

Dividends to   Julia Etheridge

Class of Share   Ordinary   **Denomination**   £1 each

Disposals	Balance	Remarks
	£1	

Register of   Directors

Surname (or Corporate Name)   Palmer
Forenames(s)   Alexander
any former Forenames or Surnames _____

Nationality   British   Date of Birth   3-2-55
Residential Address (or Registered or Principal Office   85 Preston Square
London SW6 5CN

	Date of Resignation
Other Directorships None	

Business Occupation   Company Director
Date of Appointment   3-1-99   minute   11-1-99
Date of filing particulars   3-1-99
Date of Resignation or Cessation _____ minute _____
Date of filing particulars _____

Surname (or Corporate Name)   Etheridge
Forenames(s)   Julia
any former Forenames or Surnames _____

Nationality   British   Date of Birth   29-9-57
Residential Address (or Registered or Principal Office   16 St. George's Crescent
Reading RG7 9XY

	Date of Resignation
Other Directorships WA Limited	

Business Occupation   Sales Executive
Date of Appointment   3-1-99   minute   11-1-99
Date of filing particulars   3-1-99
Date of Resignation or Cessation _____ minute _____
Date of filing particulars _____

Surname (or Corporate Name) _____
Forenames(s) _____
any former Forenames or Surnames _____

Nationality _____ Date of Birth _____
Residential Address (or Registered or Principal Office _____

	Date of Resignation
Other Directorships _____	

Business Occupation _____
Date of Appointment _____ minute _____
Date of filing particulars _____
Date of Resignation or Cessation _____ minute _____
Date of filing particulars _____

Register of   Secretaries

| Surname (or Corporate Name) Palmer |
| Forenames(s) Alexander |
| any former Forenames or Surnames |
| Date of Appointment 3-1-99 minute 11-1-99 |
| Date of filing particulars |

| Residential Address (or Registered or Principal Office) 85 Preston Square |
| London SW6 5CN |
| |
| Date of Resignation or Cessation _____ minute _____ |
| Date of filing particulars |

| Surname (or Corporate Name) |
| Forenames(s) |
| any former Forenames or Surnames |
| Date of Appointment _____ minute _____ |
| Date of filing particulars |

| Residential Address (or Registered or Principal Office) |
| |
| |
| Date of Resignation or Cessation _____ minute _____ |
| Date of filing particulars |

| Surname (or Corporate Name) |
| Forenames(s) |
| any former Forenames or Surnames |
| Date of Appointment _____ minute _____ |
| Date of filing particulars |

| Residential Address (or Registered or Principal Office) |
| |
| |
| Date of Resignation or Cessation _____ minute _____ |
| Date of filing particulars |

| Surname (or Corporate Name) |
| Forenames(s) |
| any former Forenames or Surnames |
| Date of Appointment _____ minute _____ |
| Date of filing particulars |

| Residential Address (or Registered or Principal Office) |
| |
| |
| Date of Resignation or Cessation _____ minute _____ |
| Date of filing particulars |

| Surname (or Corporate Name) |
| Forenames(s) |
| any former Forenames or Surnames |
| Date of Appointment _____ minute _____ |
| Date of filing particulars |

| Residential Address (or Registered or Principal Office) |
| |
| |
| Date of Resignation or Cessation _____ minute _____ |
| Date of filing particulars |

Register of   Directors' Interests

Name and Address of Person Interested Alexander Palmer
85 Preston Square, London SW6 5CN

Classes of Share Capital or Debentures Ordinary shares
(a) 1 share of £1 each.
(b)

No.	Entry Date	Date of Event	Date of Notification	Nature of Event	Acquisitions	Disposals	No. of Shares in which interested after event	Price consideration	Remarks
1	4-1-99	3-1-99	4-1-99	Subscriber to Memorandum of Association	1		1	£1	

Name and Address of Person Interested Julia Etheridge
16 St. George's Crescent, Reading RG7 9XY

Classes of Share Capital or Debentures Ordinary shares
(a) 1 share of £1 each.
(b)

No.	Entry Date	Date of Event	Date of Notification	Nature of Event	Acquisitions	Disposals	No. of Shares in which interested after event	Price consideration	Remarks
2	4-1-99	3-1-99	4-1-99	Subscriber to Memorandum of Association	1		1	£1	

Law Pack Publishing Limited
(Registered in England No. 1234567)

NOTICE OF EXTRAORDINARY GENERAL MEETING

NOTICE IS HEREBY GIVEN that an Extraordinary General Meeting of the above-named Company will be held at 1 James Road, London EC1 on 25th of January 1999 at 2:00 p.m. for the purpose of considering and, if thought fit, passing the following resolutions of which the resolution numbered 1 will be proposed as an ordinary resolution and the resolution numbered 2 will be proposed as a special resolution:

ORDINARY RESOLUTION

1. That the authorised share capital of the Company be and is hereby increased from £100 to £1,000 by the creation of 900 Ordinary Shares of £1 each.

SPECIAL RESOLUTION

2. That the name of the Company be changed to "Law Pack Software Limited."

BY ORDER OF THE BOARD

Secretary _____*A Palmer*_____

Dated 19th January 1999

Registered Office: 1 James Road London EC1 7OP

Note:

A member entitled to attend and vote at the Extraordinary General Meeting convened by this notice may appoint a proxy to attend and (on a poll) vote in his stead. A proxy need not be a member of the Company.

To appoint a proxy the enclosed form should be completed and deposited at the registered office of the Company not less than 48 hours before the time of the Meeting specified above or of the adjourned meeting at which the proxy proposes to vote.

LAW PACK PUBLISHING LIMITED

FORM OF CONSENT TO SHORT NOTICE
OF
EXTRAORDINARY GENERAL MEETING

We, the undersigned, being a majority in number of the Members of the Company having the right to attend and vote at the Extraordinary General Meeting of the Company to be held 25th January 1999 ("the Meeting") and together holding not less than 95 per cent in nominal value of the shares giving that right, hereby agree that the Meeting shall be deemed to have been duly convened and held and that the resolutions set out in the notice of the Meeting may be proposed and passed as ordinary and special resolutions notwithstanding that less than the requisite notice thereof as specified in the Companies Act 1985 or in the Company's Articles of Association has been given.

APalmer
_____

Alexander Palmer

Julia Etheridge

Julia Etheridge

Dated: 19th January 1999

LAW PACK PUBLISHING LIMITED

Minutes of an Extraordinary General Meeting of the Company held at 1 James Road, London EC1 on 25th January 1999 at 2.00 p.m.

PRESENT: Alexander Palmer   (Chairman)
**   Julia Etheridge**

1. The Chairman announced that a quorum was present and declared the Meeting open.

2. The Chairman announced that the necessary majority of the members of the Company had consented to the holding of the Meeting at short notice.

3. The Chairman proposed that the authorised share capital of the Company be and is hereby increased from £100 to £1,000 by creating 900 ordinary shares of £1 each and such ordinary resolution was passed unanimously.

4. The Chairman proposed that the name of the company be changed to "Law Pack Software Limited" and such special resolution was passed unanimously.

5. There being no further business, the Chairman declared the Meeting closed.

APalmer
_____
Chairman

EX/E

Company No. 1234567

COMPANIES ACT 1985
COMPANY LIMITED BY SHARES

ORDINARY AND SPECIAL
RESOLUTIONS OF
LAW PACK PUBLISHING LIMITED

(Passed 5th January 1999)

At an Extraordinary General Meeting of the above-named company duly convened and held on 25th January 1999 the following resolutions were duly passed as ordinary and special resolutions respectively:

ORDINARY RESOLUTION

1. That the authorised share capital of the Company be and is hereby increased from £100 to £1,000 by the creation of 900 ordinary shares of £1 each.

SPECIAL RESOLUTION

2. That the name of the company be changed to "Law Pack Software Limited."

APalmer

Chairman

EX/G

Company No. 1234567

LAW PACK PUBLISHING LIMITED

WRITTEN SHAREHOLDERS' RESOLUTIONS

PURSUANT TO the Articles of Association of the Company we, the undersigned being all the members of the Company entitled to attend and vote at General Meetings of the Company HEREBY AGREE AND CONFIRM that the following resolutions shall be as valid and effectual as if they had been passed as elective resolutions at a General Meeting of the Company duly convened and held accordingly we HEREBY RESOLVE:

1. THAT in accordance with the provisions of Section 252 of the Companies Act 1985 the Company hereby dispenses with the laying of accounts and reports before the Company in General Meeting in respect of the year ending 31st January 2000 and subsequent financial years.

2. THAT in accordance with the provision of Section 366A of the Companies Act 1985 the Company hereby dispenses with the holding of the Annual General Meeting for 1999 and subsequent years.

3. THAT in accordance with the provisions of Section 386 of the Companies Act 1985 the Company hereby dispenses with the obligation to appoint auditors annually and that during the term that the dispensation is in force the directors be and they are hereby authorised to fix the auditors' remuneration.

APalmer

Alexander Palmer

Julia Etheridge

Julia Etheridge

Dated: 11th January 1999

Index